YOU ARE A
DIVINE
BEING

WALWORTH NEIL

Paperback: 978-1-961438-90-3
eBook: 978-1-961438-91-0
Library of Congress Control Number: 2023917301

Ordering Information:

Prime Seven Media
518 Landmann St.
Tomah City, WI 54660

Printed in the United States of America

ACKNOWLEDGEMENT

In my long-term plans over the years, I have always considered putting some of my life experiences in writing.

That dream is now manifesting, and it is my sincere hope that my words will inspire and evoke transformation in those who read this book. This narrative is an attempt to engage the human being to acknowledge and embrace his true identity as a divine being and an extension of God.

My aim is to reach persons through my writing to enlighten them to the reality of being created in the image of God and to highlight their divinity over their humanity.

The primary motivation behind me producing this narrative is my two sons who painfully had to bury their mother, my late wife Vivette, in October of 2017. This book is the result of countless thought gathering sessions, and mountains of reflections on my life which I primarily lived for my children and their mother.

Shawn, the younger of the two sons, constantly and convincingly encouraged me to make this book a possibility. Throughout the writing process he extended his helping help as often as he could, and this helped to set me in gear.

Sheldon, our first born, was a treasure of encouragement, and he followed up on my progress at regular intervals.

My wife, Maureen, has been a tower of strength in executing this piece of writing. Her professionalism, empathy, genuine interest and motivating energy are exceedingly enriching and invaluable.

Philando, my brother, pushed me to make it happen. He applauds me for my unwavering optimism even in the face of serious challenges and pain.

Reverend Randolph Scott must also be thanked for his pastoral nurturing during the baby stage of my marriage with Vivette. The friendship and ongoing commitment he displays is very much appreciated; and he even went as far as reading the first draft of this book and offering feedback.

Glendon Watson offered tremendous support and encouragement. As an author himself, he gave me valuable advice that helped me circumvent much of the complications associated with publishing one's first book.

TABLE OF CONTENTS

INTRODUCTION

This book is not *claiming to be* a proponent of *theological* facts, religion or religious correctness. I am certainly not against organized religions because it does provide a structure as it relates to faith and beliefs. I am not writing in terms of the realms of faith, religion nor religiosity. My intention is not to be exclusive but inclusive because all humanity is created in the image and likeness of God. Even those who exclusively subscribe to humanism and hold deeply humanistic views. Whether or not you believe God, who is the creator of us all, you cannot escape Him because he made you in His image and likeness and dwells inside of you. Therefore, your religion of belief system will not distort inherent facts. – maybe elaborate further on this or state it differently. I am not sure I get the connection.

Emotions and behaviors are a component of our humanity but you transcend emotions and desires to experience a deeper divine love connection.

This narrative is simply an experience or inspirational encounter and insight that I call a divine unfolding. This kind of experience is what creates uniqueness in the inner and higher self through divine consciousness that we are sometimes unaware of. You do not necessarily have this experience while on your knees in a learned posture of prayer. Rather, it is a spontaneous outflow of loving feelings.

Many people tell their story of having similar inspirational experiences or arriving at a state of enlightenment. Some put it in songs, poems, books and chants.

This book *is the outcome of approximately four months of deep introspective reflection after the sudden passing of my late wife, Vivette, on September 10, 2017.* After careful analysis of the quality of life she lived, I became enlightened regarding the essence of human existence, and I embraced this moment of epiphany. *This story is not concerned with religion or religious feeling or beliefs. It will try to shed some light on human existence and the extent to which it syncs with divine existence.*

I entitled this book, "YOU ARE A DIVINE BEING," because this story is not about whether you are a Christian, Muslin, Rastafarian or an adherent of any other religion or faith structure. It is not about changing one's religion or religious views. It has countless references and quote from the bible, one of the most read collection of scriptures in the universe. My intent is not to push you to affirm or disagree with my writings. I am immensely aware of people's differences and diversities of views and opinions, and I think that should be respected. We all have our unique experiences and encounters in life based on our unique situations and circumstances. These encounters often bring salvation from a host of difficult circumstances.

I summed up intuitive grasp of reality and my deep transformational unfolding. It is not a re-invention of my faith but a profound enlightenment of my existence.

Inspiration means: "in spirit." (Maybe provide a source here) It is a passionate out-flow of transformative spiritual and personal encounters from deep within my innermost being. The central focus of this narrative is to demonstrate that every person is more divine than she is human. Everyone is created in the image and likeness of God, and is therefore an extension of God.

THE UNIVERSAL BEING

E very human being through divine origin entered this universe through a biological process. These biological/scientific explanations of our existence do not demystify the deep and divine origin of man. Human being came into the world after living in a closed biological space for nine months. This life was in an invisible space; the divine beginning of human existence. For nine months, this life exists in a silent womb filled with, until it finally enters our world as a newborn divine being. This process is divine and miraculous.

It transcends the human ability to genetically produce an identical copy of the human being. As mentioned earlier, human beings are created in the image and likeness of God, and science cannot perfectly replicate a divine image. It cannot be determined by the Magnetic Resource Imaging MRI. – (bit unsure what you mean here).

There is a time span that is connected to this human entry, but on the other hand, there is eternal existence in the human body. This book attempts to make clear to the conscious mind, the hidden dimension of thought as it relates to your divinity.

The intention of this book is to highlight the supernatural-ness of man. Its focus is to get the reader to make her divine self more prominent through the application of unconditional love. **It is important to** celebrate your divinity and embrace the unlimited creative divine potential that exists in the temporary human body.

The shifting of your inner energy for the development of your higher self is another highlight of this book. We should live our lives with extraordinary focus on learning and development as human beings and the deeper divine connection needs to be acknowledged and enhanced in the fullness of our existence.

This book was inspired in great part by the profound experience I had after losing my wife suddenly after over 34 years of marriage. The process of dealing with that implicit no-return reality was meditative, introspective and contemplative. It drives me to take a comprehensive look at who we are in this vast universe. It was like a Re-Invention of an existing reality of the fullness of mankind.

I was led to the invaluable acknowledge of the brevity of life. Most importantly, from that knowledge I was enlightened to the permanence of who we are as a divine being. This leads me to a Re-invention or higher consciousness of who we are as the image of God. My unrelenting shift of thought and curiosity became the source of my divine consciousness. With the resourcefulness of thought and selflessness of being it connects me to my Source-God who is always in us in paradoxical active silence. I was lead to an internal realization of my existence as a human being who can be suddenly cut off from my earthly beloved attachments and possessions.Out of those introspective thoughts it highlights the fact that my commitment, dedication and loyalty to some religion was good but was inadequate to fulfill my total divinity. There is a meeting with the divine that lives on the inside, and that transcends religion and religiosity. I am grateful for my learning and social development, but I do concede that life in its permanence is deeper and it surpasses one's social development.

The limitless nature of man is not an external achievement. The ability to love God and your neighbor as yourself is not achievable through social development nor religion. People are commonly judged by their connections, achievements, educational gains and skillsets. The intent of this manuscript is to shift that model for the path of life is meant to be one of higher consciousness and divine immersion.

Embracing the divinity of man far exceeds the task and efforts to be landed in the best job. It is not something you go to college or vocational institutions to gain. A great salesman and learned scientist, will consider themselves competent in their field of discipline based on their commitment to reached their *aspired* goal, but there is an *inspired* goal to work towards achieving.

This book is attempting to highlight the fact that there is a greater inner insight in reaching and satisfying your goal, where there is no emptiness and void but permanence and pleasure forevermore.

The question of choice is real and you can achieve the goals you desire and aspire to in life. However, if it (maybe say exactly what "it" is here) is not coming from deep within your inner self, it can later cause tremendous frustration. Man, despite significant (technological?) gain and advancement, is still experiencing emptiness. A life outside of grasping one's true self as an extension of God is one that is void of the fullness of life.

One could stay up late at nights to ensure that he covers the areas of studies to pass the required examinations for success. The question is, where does success comes from? In the process of pursuing these dreams for greatness you may neglect your family, friends and disrupt your social life as whole. Your ultimate goal is to succeed in your career path that you dreamed about. There is another neglect in the opposite direction that you should consider. You neglect your higher self and missed the ultimate Success and satisfaction of life in your higher self. – maybe reword slightly

After spending several years studying – burning the midnight oil – to secure that dream job/career, you ultimately come to realize that you do not have a passion for it. The compensation package is good, the status fits well socially but you are still dissatisfied. Suddenly your intuitive reasoning faculties force you to realize that despite all your hard work and the successful achievement of your goals, there still exists this inner vacuum. Something deep in your innermost being is telling you that something is missing from your life, or there is a mismatch between your job and your true passion. Subsequently, a revelation comes from within that your passion is music, dancing, interior decorating, or something drastically different from your current field of operation.

Even with an attractive income and a socially acceptable lifestyle, you feel unfulfilled and intrinsically dissatisfied. Your sole humanistic approach fails as it will – please clarify further.

There was this inner door that you did not open to your choice of career. You were on a human voyage without the divine pilot. You were trying to keep up with family tradition and social validations.

As parents and leaders of our children we want the best for them. We have our ideals for them as to what career path they should chose and so on. As a result, it is likely that you may have counselled, coerced or influenced them to choose a specific career path. This approach can prove dangerous or counterproductive as it relates to the children's inspiration.

Therefore, openness should be a considered when communicating with your offspring's. There exists the need to have a kind of inner consultation of the person involve in the process. – maybe remove the highlighted sentence. Parents must give good guidance but never underestimate the natural outflow of the child's supernatural endowment (maybe explain what this supernatural endowment is). Many times, what you think is unnatural is spurring a supernatural shift.

Sometimes parents see the child struggling with a particular subject that is fundamental to what they set out to achieve. Naturally you think the answer is to get some extra help for the child; this is of course not a bad move. Accordingly, you enroll your child in tutoring classes that deal with the subject in question. You are willing to sacrificially cover the cost and to change the institution of study if you think that such a change will lead to improved results. As parents we will go the extra mile to encourage and enable the success of our children. However, what about taking a pause to think and evaluate the situation more deeply? What if this field of study that the child is struggling with is not tied to her inspiration and passion?

The primary reason for the child's struggle is not necessarily a lack of ability or even accessibility to helpful resources, but rather the child's soul is leading her elsewhere. How do you find this out? One way is to just sit down and have an in-depth conversation with that child. Listen to what her heart is saying. The answers might not align with your ideals, but it is a reflection of her deep-rooted inspiration to, for example, produce music, dance, design or other activities that are not traditionally viewed as an ideal career choice.

The child only becomes a misfit when she pursues that which is not her passion, not when she fails to pursue a traditional career choice;

A person who does not have the inspired empathy to care for people may not be a great doctor or nurse or counsellor and so on. A chef puts love in cooking; a teacher puts love in teaching; an artist puts love in his artwork. They all perform at their optimum level with love as the driving force. The love comes out in their different trade and they feel self-satisfaction. This in turn makes them an inspiration to others.

There is an old saying, "you can be anything you want to be." I believe there is truth in that but what about the knowing; you want to be a doctor but the inspiration is a designer. – please clarify further.

If you reach a point where any and everything can divert you from your divine inspired path, and your work becomes tiring and laborious, it could be that you are solely motivated by economic and social validation choices. Passion and purpose may be missing. Sometimes you create your own misery by simply "being", rather than by "knowing".

You are a divine spirit created in the image of God and you must listen to the inner voice that speaks to you. What you want to be can be opposed to who you are - your higher self. When you are not fulfilling your inspired path, you can become weak and frustrated in your career choice. Consult with your inner being so that you can serve your true purpose with enthusiasm. This form of service in no way has anything to do with your choice of religion or your religious label, but rather, a full acknowledgement of your divine make up as an extension of God.

Your formal education does not define you. Your skills and aspirations must be in sync with your inspirational encounter. Your divine inspiration is the way you bring out your natural innate talent with passion and purpose to serve others and to celebrate love. Love should be the streaming frequency of your career.

Man cannot live by mere ego and leave God out of the big picture because God/Source is the originator of the total picture. Frankly, we are not merely humans; we have a higher and deeper self in our being that must dominate. That is the part of us that is filled with love and tranquility. It is transcends humanity or human-ness, and it operates in silence.

The failure to acknowledge you are a divine spirit being will likely result in you not having a joyful, fulfilled life. The question that is raised is what makes you fulfilled; Is it things or purpose? There are great many people who have a lot of material possessions but still live an unfulfilled life. You must be driven by your higher self to bring out your natural talents and abilities and achieve joy through service and everyday living. The essence of who you are goes far beyond what you have.

Some of the most successful achievers in the universe are people who pursue their naturally inspired talent in music, arts, poetry, sales, medicine, and technology to name a few. If you spend your whole life time trying to be what or who you are not you will live a dissatisfied life. Your success through the human eyes is filled with tremendous limitations. – maybe reword and/or *clarify further*

Your child's low grades in school does not necessarily mean she needs parental attention. Rather, she may just need divine intervention. Explore, investigate and invest more time in developing the child's naturally inspired potential for greatness. Greatness is in that child; a kind of greatness that academia may not readily expose. Train the child to be aware of that inner silence that is greater than his human body and is ready to unfold in her life. They will not depart from the essence of who they are.

So many of us were told what and who to be. When the motivation is to be something besides a lawyer or a doctor, ignoring that motivation can result in an unfulfilled mission. Even those that the system has designed to fail because of their race and other socio-economic status, there is a specific, deep assignment that, if completed, will lead to a life of fulfillment.

There is greatness in all of humanity. You must broaden your parental insight to grasp the divine enlightening present in the human being.

The need to advance from being a transfixed human to being transformed with a renewed mind cannot be overstated. To be transformed is to operate outside of the boundary of human confinement.

As mentioned earlier, my writing is an open-minded and inspired emergence of divine thoughts. It is not necessarily meant to be a discussion of religious doctrinal views, but a personal and divinely inspired experience that employs the divine consciousness of the supreme inner self. My writing reflects a profound thought process generated by the loss of a loved one who demonstrated divine characteristics in the face of human challenges.

Vivette, whose name means, "one who is filled with life, or gift of God, "was taken away from her human family by super natural forces that gives life and also takes it away.

This narrative is not concerned with her religion, which most certainly informed her belief system. In evaluating her life, I can safely say I was a witness of her divine graces that manifested throughout her life and shone through her human tent. She effortlessly demonstrated three-fold unconditional love to a large extent. – what does three-fold unconditional love mean?

This inspired - "in spirit" - tale is an attempt to shed light on the dichotomy of who we truly are and the fullness of our existence. The main theme of this divine reflection is to highlight the view that we are divine beings having a human experience. Put another way, we are more spirit than flesh. We are created in the image of God as an extension of God, who knew us before we were formed in our mothers' wombs.

We live in a universe of dichotomies: good and bad, love and hate, high and low, sad and happy, beginning and end, truth and lies, and so forth. The "supreme dichotomy" is that we are divine and human, capable of loving unconditionally through the God inside of us.

The supreme dichotomy acknowledges that there is a higher self and a lower self. The higher self is the soul and lower self is the body. It is easy for us to look on the outer man for the answer to who we are because tremendous emphasis is placed on the material rather than the spiritual. Labels are placed on people based on their socioeconomic status and their academic or professional achievements.

If your life centers solely around your social, economic and educational gains, when those things are gone you will be reduced to nothing. You are in reality a limitless, weightless, eternal being that existed before the formation of the world. Life is this wonderful divine gift that has many definitions by different people and philosophers but primarily we are a divine soul; an extension of God living in a human body. We are all living organisms that are capable of responding to stimuli and can create life through reproduction and divine transformation.

Life is eternal, weightless, limitless and supernatural. It is intended to be driven by love. This divine phenomenon transcends the human explanation as the involvement of the supernatural is highly mysterious.

In the book of Timothy 3:16 , it states "Beyond all question, the mystery from which godliness springs is great: He (God in Jesus form) appeared in the flesh, was vindicated by the spirit, was seen by angels, was preached among the nations was believed on in the world, was taken into glory"

Life goes far beyond the physical body. Its meaning is enveloped in the divine. It is through your inner and higher self you find the true meaning of life. Jesus, the God/man, expresses this notion when he states: "I am the way, the truth and the life." As a divine, limitless, borderless representation of God in the flesh, Jesus exposed the truth of His infiniteness.

Psalm 139:14 points out that you are "...fearfully and wonderfully made." This literally means that you are an awesome wonder. Human perception is incapable of fully explaining or completely capturing who you truly are.

This is an inspired manuscript of our human and divine interconnection and interdependence, highlighting that Human beings are not merely flesh. Rather, we are immersed into love because we are all created by love. It is a book that directs you to your true inner divine self that is eternal, invisible and made in the image of our source God. One highlight of this material is the recall to the conscious mind, real living from the innermost being. It establishes the fact that we are more spirit than flesh and that we are divine beings.

The human body is the outer temporary self with tremendous limitations, while our divine self is invisible, limitless, weightless and infinite. We are all divine eternal beings that are under divine influence. The intensification of this inner life leads to true refuge in God, the source. God is that invisible divine presence that is always in our lives.

Man cannot exist outside of the presence of God because God is present everywhere: within every Human being and every time and space for all eternity. Psalms 139:9-10 states that "If I take the wings of the morning, and dwell in the uttermost parts of the sea, God's hand is there to hold me". We are equipped with human senses - tasting, smelling, hearing, feeling and seeing. These human senses are necessary for you operate in your present form. God, our Source, says before you were formed in your mother's whom he knew you and he will never leave you.

Clearly, we exist even before our mother and father get together and conceived for the purpose of our human entry into this universe.

The body changes as we grow. This change is referred to as the life cycle. The divine soul, however, never changes. In fact, it is eternal. To advance our being we must be true to who we really are and embrace this mysterious dichotomy of human and divine.

Jesus in the New Testament remains consistently true to who he was as a divine being clothed in a human body. When Jesus was present in human flesh, He accentuated His divinity and de-emphasized His humanity.

How can we make our divinity over our humanity more prominent and more noticeable? The single answer is to let love from our being flow effortlessly. Jesus said "I am the vine!" No fruit is produced unless there is connection to the vine. As you change *you* and adopt the divine attitude, *you* change your love vibration. Man is God's power at work as expressed by God's statement that "I am that I am". Your divine mental attitude is the creative entrance to love, peace and joyful well-being.

Affirm that you are more divine that human and that will open the door of a conscious union between you and the God inside of you. You are in partnership with the divine God source. God is in us as this divine omnipresent being who energizes us to make our divinity prominent. "I am" is your true identity that connects you to the true nature of God.

They crucified Jesus for affirming that he is divine and operates in partnership with God. In the book of John 10:33, in the New Testament, they accused Jesus of blasphemy; the Jews said to Jesus "For a good work we will not stone you, but for blasphemy because you being a man is making yourself God".

The Jews' arguments were legally motivated but Jesus was speaking from a divine position. There is absolutely no need to be fearful of confidently affirming that you are not only human but also a divine being. Make that declaration and affirmation that you are a divine extension of God. It may not be a popular or accepted position but it is a surrender to your perfection in the divine.

Jesus was not making himself God. He was always God in human flesh. Jesus was the prototype for every human being that comes through the birth canal. In verse 30, of St. John chapter 10 He said "I and My Father are One". In verse 34-35 He states: "Is it not written in your law, I have said you are gods". If he calls them gods, unto whom the word of God came, and the scripture cannot be broken." Jesus lived and manifested His Divinity in his human tent. He was totally in-spirit in his human experience and appearances.

This book has no set of rules to live by, nor is it an attempt to change who you are or the rules/laws you live by. It is about leading you to divinely validate who you are. Rather than acting as a dogmatic doctrine, this book is an inspired narrative for expanding your consciousness to know your Source God and be the true reflection of Him as a divine spirit. This is a didactive project and conversation to take you from merely believing to knowing who God is and so as to develop the awareness that he is living in you. This is not a call to join a church and cling to a particular denomination. God exists is in every human being under the sun with no geographical, social, economic, ethnic or religious exemption.

Never doubt your ability to know God because He is alive in you as that inspired presence that enables you to love from your higher self. Humanity is sensory and fragile but divinity transcends limitations; it is infinite and eternal. It is not about over-ruling to decide against any other view, but it aims to offer a spiritual autobiography of your divine self.

It is important that we establish an over-arching link to who we truly are as human beings in this universe. This narrative was inspired to share and expand the truth that "as a man thinketh in his heart so is he/she". It is about opening your mind to its limitless potential and aims to encourage and advance readers' consciousness surrounding their godly nature..

It is a freedom call from human bondage and from Leonardo Da Vinci's historically inaccurate portrait of Jesus as a blond hair, blue eyed man. Through enlightenment the thinking that one race is superior to the other can be eradicated. You, no matter your race, creed or color, are created in the image and likeness of God and is an extension of God. Furthermore, God is love and we are divine partners with God.

It is significant to make it known that I am not writing as a scholar or theologian. I am simply a vehicle or a conduit who is putting forth the point to acknowledge your divinity. Let your life be lived from a deeper inner intimate reality so as to embrace your existence in totality while ensuring that you are not disconnected from you creator.

As Jesus puts it in the New Testament "I am the vine and you all are the branches". The vine cannot produce foreign branches. We are all divine beings, controlled and inspired in our soul by the divine source - the vine.

The vine cannot be different in nature from the branches. An apple tree can only produce apples, it cannot produce plum or any other kind of fruit.

The Apostle Paul encourages us to "be transformed by the renewing of [our] mind[s]". To be transformed means that you are operating outside of your limitations; you are not confined by human boundaries.

The first and greatest commandment encourages us to "love the Lord your God with all your soul and with all your mind and strength" and the second states clearly "love your neighbor as yourself." The first and second commandments establish the ultimate principle that we should live by. All the other commandments hang on these two commandments.

In order to demonstrate these principles, we must know ourselves through the divine connection as the extension of God. It cannot be attained in its fullness through the human self. You must surrender human ego and cling to the meekness of heart live through your higher self.

This book is most definitely not to tell you that your religion is wrong or right, nor to put away whatever label it carries or doctrine it advances.

This is to raise your consciousness and divine understanding of who you truly are. This unfolding is rooted in the spirit world that is not entirely removed from you because we are all created as a divine spirit that exists in human flesh.

It is not to be understood as a human being living in the spirit but as a spirit living in human frame. This is a path to knowing God instead of believing in God because whether you believe in God or not it does not change the truth that God exists in every human being. Even atheists and agnostics have God present inside of them. They are created in His image and likeness. God will never leave you nor forsake you because of your human weaknesses because His relationship with humanity is unconditional.

As I have mentioned before, this book came to be after deep introspection and reflection following the passing of my late wife Vivette. This story is much about relationship; it is important to mention that we are part of an inevitable social network existing as interdependent beings.

God created a network of human beings whom He knew very well before we were even formed in our respective mothers' wombs. His divine guidance dwells in you working through you during the course of your life. To recognize these guiding principles, you need to establish a covenant with love. Love connects you to your divine and higher self.

The New Testament of the bible says we must love our neighbor as we love ourselves.

In the marriage vows it said the two shall be one flesh. As denoted by our customized fingerprints, we are all unique individuals. Yet, when placed in an intimate relationship, the two becomes one. To consciously come to grip with this relationship with our Source we must operate from the God inspired department of our being. In order to love your neighbor as you love yourself you have to dwell in the realm of love. Love is a soul energy generated from the divine source who is the summation of all love. Your human ego will fight to restrict the overturn the decision to love God and your neighbor as you love yourself.

The accentuation of inner life will help to shift you from the physical and material self. It will elevate you from the human flesh that is changing constantly and is limited and fragile to a vital spiritual wholeness. You must operate in the spirit realm to have real understanding of your being more divine than human. Because of the eternal nature and limitlessness of your divinity, the goal to forgive and love unconditionally is achievable.

Love must be the cheerleader; the epicenter; the creme de la crème of your life. There is no room for hate and resentment in your relationships.

Letting go of ego you are enabled to operate from a deep divine devotion. Jesus in human flesh intensified His divinity during his 33 years on the earth. He was devoted to saving humanity through love and with love. He confidently told us to love our enemies. In order to accomplish that you must rise above your human self and achieve divine consciousness. Human focus is centered on ego and the concept of who is right and who is wrong. Loving your enemies has nothing to do with who is wrong or right. It is a demonstration of unconditional love.

Experiencing the beauty and joy of relationships requires a full surrender of human ego. It is extraordinary how human beings wake up each day with hate and resentment in their hearts just because they hold different beliefs. It happens through religion, politics and race relations and the choice of who you chose to be your partner, just to name some of the plethora of reasons there exists a divide among humankind. Is it not ok to have a different belief or point of view from another individual?

When you are in a relationship there is no vacancy for resentment, but there should always be room for different views and beliefs. It does not matter the nature of the relationship; we are not monolithic beings. You must establish, maintain and broadcast from a frequency of love. The intensification of this love finds its beauty and value in the divine inner self.

You must treasure and preserve the virtues to be kind rather than right in dealing with your spouse, friend and your neighbor.

Relationships cannot be about control, although they come with conflicts. It is not about a passive approach to life but an active engagement of unconditional love. It should be a complimentary commitment and union built on understanding. When the inevitable conflict, disagreement or error occurs, do not explain away your infractions or mistakes. Instead, open a conversation with the aim of ultimately finding resolutions.

The cause and the effect of the infractions is done and becomes a thing of the past. That past event cannot be removed or eliminated, but you can build a wholesome attitude going forward for the purpose of sustaining that relationship.

Have conversations in love and by love, which is the ultimate glue that a person can use to mend any relationship. You can't use caustic words as the transport to the destination of resolution. You ever pause to wonder why simple things like burning the toast or leaving a pair of socks on the floor sometimes result in a big argument? Sometimes the way we talk to our love ones in a conflict is problem. We need to pause, rethink and ask ourselves the question, "Am I in love?" "Do I love my neighbor as I love myself". Simple actions or inactions can mushroom into great conflicts that turns into ego conflicts. Can we not make love be that scarlet thread that runs through our relationships? Why are we so quick to judge when dealing with one another?

It is spiritually myopic to pass judgement on anyone for any reason. Your role is to build up each other and not to judge. How does one provide the answer to the question: am I a part of the peace or a promoter of conflicts? To answer that question, you must open that door to your inner self and seek insight from a deeper place.

Jesus said in the New Testament, "Judge not." Just expand your thoughts to a place where you can discover the divine intelligence in the situation in question or contention. Judgement is a prejudice position to take. Love is the single spectacle to use to view a human being in his divine self, he/she is better than what you are seeing and hearing. The most conspicuous evidence of man's actions is ego. Ego is at work when you take revengeful actions against another human being because they disagree with you or say something about you that you don't approve of. Behind that ego there is the divine or "deeper good" in you that encourages you to pause for a moment and say to yourself, "that's merely their opinion of me."

There is a higher power that is directing your life but ego will drown it out with self-seeking approvals. The divine presence in you is always guiding and directing you to the unconditional love approach. Who do people listen to? The inner deeper you or the ego? Egotistical actions have become the order of the day. In the past, from a practical sense, people would go to a priest, pastor or other clergy individuals for answers but now we find that they gravitate to individuals in other professions for solutions. For example, nowadays when one begins to consider divorce he/she tends to bypass the "people of the cloth" and instead seek out a divorce lawyer. Man is always looking for answers outside of divine conscience because he is ego oriented.

You do not know enough to place judgement on a person who may accuse you wrongfully or who makes an inaccurate evaluation of you. Stop for a moment and think why he or she is making that judgement call? It is never your business to impose your value- judgement or opinion on other people. God requirement is for you to love unconditionally and leave judgement to Him who offer love before and in judgement.

Judgement is God's prerogative. Such a being is the only source that is qualified to judge man. The discernment of the intent of your heart and soul is His competence. You don't know the person's life experiences; you have never experienced their trauma. How well can you judge them when you do not know the hurt and pain they endured? To a large extent the white man cannot feel the pains the black man experiences at the hands of racism. How can you know how it feels to be discriminated against when you or your forefathers and mothers has not had that experience? No man knows enough about any man to judge him or her. The main common connection we have with each other is divinity. Culture, color, social and geographical differences should not be a barrier to the divine, higher consciousness because we are all a part of God.

Do not carry resentment. It is a heavy weight on the human heart that will destroy your tent. The acknowledgement of the uniqueness of the individual and divine love for humanity will enable wholesome relationships.

Your mandate is to love unconditionally. This is not saying you should succumb to inaction but to be empathetic towards your neighbor. Find that divine energy deep inside of your being that pushes you to love unconditionally. This doesn't mean that all of your neighbors are your friends, but they are all an extension of the one and only God who lives in you and in them.

Sometimes it is your very parents/guardians and loved ones who hurt you. How do you come out of that without deep resentment? The only overwhelming conquering energy is unconditional love. That will enable you to see the person who hurt you as a work of art that is unfinished. Enter into your higher self and draw upon that frequency of forgiveness. The spontaneous influence of you action will depend on what you have on the inside. Peace and affectionate love are profoundly embedded in your soul. Try to insulate yourself from offence so as not to be offended by another people's opinion of you. Directing offensive opinions towards someone is a form of judgment. You can only be offended if you go around accepting other people's opinions of who you are. Know you are more than a mere human.

Offence is a self-initiated. No one can impose an offensive opinion on you unless you choose to accept their view of you. Such an opinion is not a reflection of who you truly are. It is their opinion and it is based on very limited information. That opinion should be treated as "fake news." The art of loving your neighbor as your self is in part how you respond to things like these. Protecting ego will allow you to react with defiance and even retaliate with violence.

Instead of resenting them and retaliating, be open to learn from anything they say that could cause that resentment. Wholesome relationships have much to do with self-esteem and self-worth. Try to preserve and maintain your own self-worth and self- esteem. It is called self-esteem and self-worth because it is an initiative that you have control over.

Many times past hurt destabilizes you and push you to think less of yourself. Simply rise to your higher self to overcome with that divine support on the inside. Most, if not all, times people place the wrong labels on others because they are coming from a human standpoint.

There is a common saying, "what you are speak so load I need not as any question". That can be true but, on the other hand, it can be a prejudice position that hampers one's ability to accurately analyze and determine the truth about someone else; in effect, "you cannot judge a book by its cover".

However, when you operate as your divine higher self you radiate a dazzling light of hope that brightens our world. You then start living a life outside of the norm. Countless people will admire you as you overwhelm your fellow humans with love and care. There exists a kind of socialization where people tend to accept toughness. They romanticize a world where to be tough makes you look strong. I am of the perspective that looking tough is the greatest sign of weakness.

God knew you before you enter this realm called Earth in human form. He is the only competent Spirit that can truly judge you accurately because he judges you by love and in love. Remember, you are a divine being having a human experience so you are dealing with human failing attitudes and actions. In that fragile human frame, however, exists the power and presence of God that encourages us to pursue righteousness.

As a result of this truth, all human beings can show love but this love must be initiated from a divine inner self. This long and difficult journey of *loving your enemies and neighbors as you love yourself requires the application of love without prejudice.* See the powerful divine image of God in all humans and . dismiss all hate from your innermost being. God aides you to love your neighbor as you love yourself. You must make a commitment desperately to love who you are in order to love others and do unto others as you would have them do to you.

Your thoughts are the most powerful intangible tool God gave you to be who you are.

Be diligent and conscious of the thoughts you welcome because "as a man thinketh in his heart so is he". Seeing yourselves as a divine being will enable you to overcome the hurdles in relationships.

In relationships, embed your energy and thought with love for humanity. You have God on your inside and that is everything you need to live in harmony with others and to love your fellow humans. See the goodness of God in your spouse, partner, friends and neighbors. Do not try to change the person in your human flesh, just send them love because love covers all the defects.

Avoid all thought that will cause stress and doubt, believe in yourself and in others. See each other as a divine being (God/Good/Virtue in each person. Changing your thoughts or perspective about your mate and others will change your whole world.

God sees you as the "apple of His eye" It is important for us to see others as God sees them. They all need that divine love and to be seen as individuals with special virtuous possibilities.

There is someone living in you that is greater than you. The Bible said; "Be transformed by the renewing of your mind". Never give your relationship a time out period. Identify God's presence in your loved ones. . Practice giving love even if it is not returned to you.

Never let what you do not know get you into a wrong mood, get you to make a wrong move or say the wrong things. Make conscious choices that will benefit the relationship. Choose to have good health, be rich, be happy, be grateful and enjoy divine abundance. "Let the weak say I am strong". "Let the poor say I am rich." Every existence begins in your soul with thoughts you can't see but it exists in you with transforming forces and tremendous possibilities.

Let happiness be the way of life, not only an emotion. Make the resolution to be happy; it is your birthright.

Open the door to your inside to find that joy of living each day. Build and mold your life with joyful enthusiasm, it will enhance your health and abundant life. Never be disappointed with the choice you make, even if you discover that you were in a hurry at the time. It's all a part of

God's plan. Learn from it. Imagine the life you want to live and visualize it.' Jesus did it with tremendous success and incalculable achievement. During his human journey, while in the midst of experiencing intense human pain Jesus said to his divine father, "If it is possible let this bitter cup pass from me, nevertheless not according to my human will but let your divine will be done". Paul further solidifies Jesus' notion when he encouraged us to "say to these things that are not, as if they were."

Reach for the moon since your life is filled with countless possibilities thanks to your divinity. Strive to achieve excellence and enthusiasm over evil thoughts.

Abraham Maslow put forth the "Self-Actualization", theory, which is based on a humanistic perspective. However, there is also divine self-actualization you must aspire to. Never lose sight of the fact that you are created and endowed with pure love that enabled you to love your neighbor as you love yourself.

Listen to the inner voice within you that your mate cannot hear. Operate your life from the inside. It is your soul that's the divine you. Your soul is an instructor; that inner you that is in touch with your source/God. Your love will destroy your anxieties and replace it with peace and kindness. Give your divine- self priority and be God-minded. "Be anxious for nothing'. Always remember "All things are possible with God" and He is always present. The soul needs divine surrender to construct the outcome of your desires. Your desires are resources in you, coming from a divine source who promised to grant you the desires of your heart.

THE PARADIGMS OF EGO AND FORGIVENESS

Self-importance can be a distractor, destroyer and a distorter of soul truth and divine favors. Have an internal dialogue as you draw from divine intelligence and reached deep into your soul when ego wants to take control. Can we truly live from our ego? Can we forgive those who even deliberately hurt us?

You have divine energy that is so transforming it will enable you to focus on solutions rather than problems. Make your challenges or problems be a teachable moment. Divine love is the author and transporter of forgiveness. It is that all sufficient grace that will bring you true results with a blissful impact in your life.

Forgiveness is a soul and God method that is available in abundance to service and soothe your relationships.

First forgive yourself and you will find it easy to forgive others. Forgiveness has no recurring sanction; we all have that divine energy gushing through us like a stream in the desert. It deletes the infraction from your human computer and places trust in your soul software. Find something in the relationships that inspire you and every inactive force in you will come alive. What you are not certain of for sure will put you in a place of doubt that is no stage to perform on. Your thoughts must be able to be validated and come out real because doubt is a dividing phenomenon. The right measuring stick to any situation you are confronted with is divine love. Release everything in your relationship to your inner dialogue before you have a conversation with your loved one about any conflict or misunderstanding.

Evict guilt out of your life and take a divine stroll and tell God about what is bothering you. Be honest and open because these distractions are found in the biological depth of your being.

The divine love and honesty will remove distractions and illuminate your path to solutions. Do not dwell on the past; the past is irreversible and unattainable; it is gone and you will never see it again.

It is widely accepted that the only thing that is constant in life is change. Esteem the present because the present is your tool to work with.

Always end a conflict with love. Your conflict must give birth to more love instead of resentment and animosity. Do not open the door to ego conflict. See conflict as an opportunity to open a conversation seasoned with love.

Most conflicts in relationships are pseudo conflicts. These kinds of conflicts are not real but imaginary; O they appear real. Be people-oriented even in the midst of a conflict, whether with a spouse, children friends, and neighbors. Choose to be kind over to be right. It is always more rewarding to be kind over being right. Aspire to make your life an inner-self working of art that paints magnificent pictures of love that makes all experiences meaningful. Reach to the frequency that let your motives be constructed out of care and concern for the well-being of your relationships.

As I have stated before, there is a divine intelligence in every encounter in your life, even in suffering. I am not saying suffering is good, I am asserting that in spite of that assignment, divine intelligence is available through it.

Fill yourself with love, care, kindness, peace and meekness as these are the means by which we draw on that indomitable divine spirit.

These qualities will then begin to surface when you are faced with vicissitudes. If you are filled with love and kindness these traits will come out when you are squeezed by ego-conflict and arrogance. Apple juice cannot come out of a mango, and, on the contrary, mango juice cannot come out of an apple. What you have inside of you will come out of you if someone or something squeezes hard enough you. Suppose another motorist runs your car off the road, what naturally come out of you? Is it peace, kindness, and goodness? Do not let any ill-communication come out of your mouth towards that person/motorist. Rather, live peaceably with all humanity and send love to fellow human beings.

Do not curse the dark as you are a divine being who is, the Light in the darkness. You can naturally shine in any dark situation that life has to offer and illuminate other people's lives.

Doctor Martin Luther King Jr. points out that *"you cannot see the stars unless it is dark."* Remember God said 'it is not what comes out of you defiles you, it is what you put in'. Never let ego overtake you – instead 'be transform by the renewing of the mind' as the Apostle Paul said in the New Testament.

Since you love your friends, spouse, children and neighbor, speak of love at all times, even in disagreements. Let love be your divine mantra. Sometimes when we talk to each other and what comes out of our mouth does not sound like love. We should strive to let our conversations be seasoned with love.

God is love, and God's love is the greatest gift to all mankind. It gives collective and communal life to man's existence. The actions of Love supersedes all other actions, gifts and all other acts of goodness This is because love is meant to be the foundation of all actions. Love is kind and it should be the driving force behind every human interaction Love should be an outflow of enthusiasm.

Enthusiasm is an expression of "The God in you". Loving from the God center of your being will enable you to achieve enthusiastic love. Love for your fellow human beings, including your enemies, illustrates the divine consciousness of your total being. This is not a religious proposition, it is simply an instruction manual for living through your higher self.

Being egocentric is poisonous to relationships. Operating from a position of selfishness and the failure to be other-oriented is of little or no benefit to anyone else. You should live and let love be the defender, protector and keeper of your relationships. There is no need to be overly competitive as we are all in partnership with God for the good of all humanity. You do not need to win the fights that arise, instead employ empathetic listening because no battle is won in the flesh nor by promoting ego. God said the battle is His!

It comes with tremendous rewards being a peacemaker as it provides bridges and not walls. You are a partaker of divine nature and peace is the best weapon to establish solutions to conflicts and ego-related problems. Peace manifests God's essence to the universe against the backdrop of gentle kindness. Your peacemaker role is not to physically avoid conflict. It is to use that legacy that Jesus left with all humanity to foster soberness and solace amongst others.

Submit to your inner divine intention to construct wholesome relationships. Do not promote nor accentuate limitations by saying things that will not enhance healthy relationships. It's better to say "we will always have wholesome conversations." Set about to change that conception that peace is not possible. That is only a plausible excuse to perpetuate ego conflict.

You ever wake up one day and watch the morning news and it would appear as if there is this urgency to commit evil and atrocities across many parts of the world? You may even say what a dangerous and wicked world to live in.

I am submitting in this book that this is not a wicked world. I It is a beautiful world that sends peace and love through nature in the atmosphere. It is a world that is under supernatural control. Saint James in the New Testament said the "tongue is an unruly member that is difficult to tame." Therefore, we should temper what we speak and weigh what comes out of our mouths. Let what comes from your tongue be with a divine thought based on love. Can we see perfection in this creation? Is there perfection when we walk in the grass and see the stream flow into the ocean and the trees sheltered under the canopy of heaven?

There is an outburst of perfection in nature and in all humanity. How can one use this unruly tongue to be a supreme vehicle of peace and love? How do you deploy and engage love in such turmoil and conflict that you see in the world and even in your own relationships with your fellow man?

We should see our loved ones as our universal neighbors in the way Solomon the author of Songs of Solomon , suggests in Chapter 8:; "Place me like a seal over your heart, as a seal upon your arm, for love is as strong as death… Love burns like blazing fire, like a mighty flame; many waters cannot quench love; river cannot wash love away. If you give all the wealth of your house (heart, soul) for love, it would be utterly scorned (angered, cursed, bad-mouthed.)" Never speak bad things or have evil thoughts or scorn about your relationship.

Let love be your character and the theme of your actions because love is who you are. God is love and God is in you. Therefore, you have that divine energy that evokes that divine love. Love must be placed on perpetual exhibition in your daily lives.

Live with increasing gratitude for the unparallel gift of love. Love is of God and God's love is preserved within your innermost being. Let your soul hear the silence of unconditional love in your speech and in the way you live. Let your voice of unconditional love be a garden of flowers that your loved ones can walk into and pick flowers to adorn the anxieties. Elevate misunderstandings to a strength discussion to find common ground in your relationships. Customize your love with divine display. Have careful discussion with spouses, children, friends and neighbors over sensitive topics rather than recklessly risking your relationships. Give reassurance to your loved ones for who they are. Don't push them to be who you want them to be.

Close up any wound and scars in your relationships with love. Whatever created those differences, expunged them from your long-term memory and give peace the chance to work through you in silent empathy. Get the sting out of your bite by destroying the venom of resentment and anger.

When a bee or wasp bite you, it is not the bite that cause the prolong swelling and pain, it is the sting that remains in you. Do not go to sleep with the sting in you, apply some divine iodine; have a conversation with your loved ones. Temper the tendency to use monologues to arrive at amicable compromise. Keep love awake to steer away from ego and fallacious conclusions.

Solomon states, in Songs of Songs Chapter 5:2, "I slept but my heart was awake; listen! My lover is knocking."

Invest loving (or active?) listening in all your relationships, it will unfold monumental returns. Let your conversation sound like love, weigh your words with kindness. When eagerness and enthusiasm generate your frequency – God joins you and expands your bandwidth to reach resolution. Boost your divine Wi-Fi of love so that your neighbors can pick up the signal coming through with high frequency. Awake and expand the sleeping divinity inside of you – God is a present help when it seems like you are in a predicament. Let enthusiasm be your inspiring tool. Embrace your divinity with identifiable sincerity. It is the God in you showing up to divide the 'Red Sea' and give you free passage to your promised land of excellence.

Remember, no one is like you. We are all unique. Be sensitive to the feeling of others and love with inner intensity "The Living God is in you engaging you to forged a good relationship and positively reinforce the other person. Tell your inner-self that you know, not only believe, that with God all things are possible

Make a resolve to view yourself not as a mere human, but also as a divine procreator with the ability to have a great impact on the growth and well-being of others. You are the only person that can change you.

It is futile to try to change other people, they themselves must resolve to want the change. Your role is to have that inner divine dialogue. You can certainly create the environment and opportunity for others to take a deep introspective look and open the door on the inside to change their thinking.

Avoid the excuse that the way you are is just who you are because it is hereditary. You are a divine being with transformational possibilities. You are under divine leadership that will enable positive changes and an opportunity to grow beyond your human self.

Proverbs 3:5-6 states "Trust in the Lord with all your heart and lean not on your own understanding. In all your ways acknowledge Him and He will direct your paths." Affirm what you want in and from your relationships. Example: like "I am enjoying this relationship I want it; I am loving it". "As a man thinketh in his heart so is he"; "Say to those things that are not as though they are. (Rom.4:7) God is in you and creates new inspirational development moments daily.

Because of your divine connection with the all-powerful God, you have a compelling energy in you to manifest divine qualities. The over investment in your humanity can interfere with one's ability to connect to a meaningful divine consciousness. Reigniting the divine prominence will come with human struggles.

St. Paul kind of addressed these struggles in his own life. He saw himself as 'a wretched man'. However, Jesus said to Paul, "leave it to me," my grace is sufficient; my strength is made perfect in your struggles". There is no excuse to blame yourself for any deficiency. God made paid provision for your overwhelming ability to work with who you are in Jesus's example. He died for your victory in life and even in death. You can ultimately put to death your humanness and transcend to divinity.

Be enthusiastic about your life, affirm that the God in you is making your life wonderful to fulfill His good pleasure. God is not weary or tired of working with you even if humans give up on you. He is at the forefront of your struggles, that is why He called himself "the vine" and mankind is "the branches". When the boisterous winds of life come upon you, He is your stabilizing support. He is so very much in you, sharing that common divinity. These struggle experiences are to change your life course to be a rigorous thinker working towards divine fulfillments. This is a way of re-entering your deeper being to come up with winning strategies.

Your strategies should be a renewal of you God consciousness. They should help to eliminate every thought that come to infiltrate you or to persuade you accept defeat You should embrace a position of victory even when facing difficult circumstances.

Remember, no battle belongs to you – and it is never physical.. Every battle that is fought on the divine battleground will result in assured victory . We are human spectators watching and observing the divine/ soul making us into overwhelming conquerors. As an occupant in the human body you will be confronted with many difficult battles. In these times you need to enter your higher self to find resolve, and embrace silence as a spectator. Be alert to detect devices and destroy them in the battleground of your mind.

Employ silence in your life. It is the way God speaks to you. When you enter that closet of silence, you partner with that divine source. Listen to the divine you, as well as your peers and loved ones. You should surrender to empathetic listening. In the moments of divine silence, you will have unfolding insights. This will enrich your soul, enable you to operate from that higher frequency, and activate sound conversation; a conversation that will sway you from an ego trip.

The past will try to emerge in the midst of any battle presenting a relationship conflict. It will try to contrast your journey to resolution with where you were.

Where you were then should be viewed as a part of your training for developing and maintaining wholesome relationships. Now move into action strategies to confront the now with a positive divine attitude.

Can you get into the habit of holding on to your opinion until you are supplied with facts? What about listening to the other person in silence, and reinforcing that individual even if you disagree with them? Affirm your understanding of what the other is saying. Your understanding and confidence in that person will energize him/her to listen with openness to learn and even adapt. This is empathetic listening, not clouded with judgement.

We learn in silence and facilitate growth through difficult conversations. It is God's supernatural game plan. Always recognize that others are not like you and they don't need to be. It is quite likely that their perspective of the situation may frustrate you especially if you have a perfectionist mindset that is weighted in particular moral or social values. Be open to build rather than tear down by simply listening to the other person with an open mind.

There is a supernatural power in you that will enable you to combat the forces of the past that will judge you. . You have help. Hold your point and listen for a little longer. The God in you is working in silence with you. You are equipped with all the resources to build wholesome relationships with even those who are different and who embrace different views

Remember to affirm what Jesus said in the Gospel of the New Testament: "All that is thine is mine." That divine power and authority is very present within you. By embracing that knowledge, you will determine and evoke that power in you to build good relationships. Consciously affirming that truth will enlighten you and help see to it that you do not succumb to the desire to merely win an argument. Strength and meekness are in silence.

Elevate your divinity with complete inner consciousness that is ever present within all circumstances.

Circumstances don't determine who you are but they do enable you to become a better person through divine assistance. Your circumstances are capacity building tools to strengthen you.

So many times, you find yourself in situations that you cannot change by yourself. Rather, you require deep inner consultation to take action.

Jesus stated in the New Testament; "I and my father are one".". Be one with your creator and work with Him, He is God-, God is Love. Affirm yourself so that you will be able to affirm others. Don't aspire to be the best religious class., Aspire to be that source of love you would associate with a divine being; that profound acknowledgement and extension of God. Love is that power in you that will point you to victory over your present situation. You actually make a human paradigm shift to a divine synchronicity in your relationship with God. This shift will free you from egocentrism.

In a world where racism and classism are a common feature, where you are measured and merited by your skin color, you need to use love as the awareness strategy to work with. From that position you can give voice to the voiceless.

The acknowledgement of the power of love is the acknowledgement of God at work in you. It will point you to victory over your present situations.

RELATIONSHIP AND RESENTMENT

A sk yourselves the following questions: is resentment advancing relationships?; What is resentment? The primary meaning of resentment is "bitter indignation; it stems from being treated unfairly." Resentment can cause one to feel less than worthy, and may bring forth other mixed emotions. Can one live without resentment? Does it benefit either party in any relationship?

Every successful relationship is selfless and other-oriented, and is punctuated with love and kindness. To dispel egocentric behavior in your relationships there must be a presumption of resentment free.

That presumption is a demonstrated consciousness that you are not merely a human being. When you are confronted or overshadowed with human challenges, it creates mixed emotions including hate and resentment. Your situations can be changed through the unique existence of the divine spirit deep inside of your physical body. Think for a moment and take a pause; you can completely destroy relationships with the plague of ego and resentment. Resentment is a weakness that needs to be managed but most of us struggle to be strong enough to use love to conquer even systemic hurts.

Resentment will deactivate the spiritual energy and drive of your inner being and deteriorate your physical body. Resentment is a residual anxiety that is an outburst of ego. Where does resentment and hate come from? These anxieties and bitterness comes to you from many sources. These include social and ethnic prejudice, class. characteristic of that dish out indignant displeasure and insults.

It is uncharacteristic of your divinity to create or harbor anger and allow it to grow and spread wildly in your relationships.

It is unreasonably excessive how through selfish ego and stereotypical outplay one acts in contempt of others who are different from them or share different views, or are born with a different skin color.

Why do you make enemies of others because they share a different religion or political worldview? People promote and perpetuate inhumane behaviors to others because of their own life choices, where they come from, where they live and their social class. You are all created in the image of God and are an extension of that divine Source.

Negative behaviors are not characteristic of living from your higher self. That is totally living from an egocentric stereotypical form, void of your divine consciousness to love unconditionally.

God gave us a perfect universe with its miraculous wonders, including the human being who is perfect in divinity. By promoting his humanity over his divinity man creates helter-skelter through race, religion, class and politics. He shifts God's perfection with unwholesome thinking and devious actions and beliefs. Why not give "knowing" priority over your beliefs? Open the door on your inside to know!

Humanity gives more credit to the human self than the divine self. Can you overcome the evil in this world?

To prevail against the evil in our world you have to find the power that exists in you to overcome your pain and hurt. So many people were captured and literally robbed of their identities, then placed in a strange place as fugitives.

No battle must be fought with the physical but rather with divine consciousness. Look on your inside for results and overwhelming victory. Spare no effort to find the freedom within your being. Divine issues can only be fixed with divine energy of love and enthusiasm.

Life is a constant lesson with divine intent. Our thoughts must keep us in the mindset that is consistent with Peter's words in the New Testament: "gird the loin of your mind". God says: "In all your ways acknowledge him and he will direct your path." Open up yourself to the unstoppable potential inside your soul. Your divine self is that unviewable, weightless and undefinable you that observes you in all ways to weaken all inconsistencies. Open your thoughts and mind to your divinity and live beyond your human limitations.

Love the God in you with all that you are, with all your heart, all your mind, all your strength. God expects you to love yourself because that is the formula to love your neighbor; especially those who used and abused you and still perpetuate these inhumane acts through systemic establishments.

There is a song that expresses that "Love is like a magic penny, give it away it comes right back to you." The more love you give the more love comes back to you to enable your freedom. Love is a gentle silent energy that flows and ignites the universe. This with a flame of acknowledgement, acceptance and approbations. The universe is filled with God's presence through love. All humanity has that common capacity to love but many times this capacity is not often displayed.

As I have said before, Jesus said my father and I are one. They crucified him for that profound truth, but he maintained that factual account of His claim throughout eternity.

Humanity has to be open to that divine claim and live honorably while abiding by that undeniable truth. Self-love already exists, in you just have to remain aware of this and accept that divine implant. Start giving away love and it will come back to you endlessly and effortlessly. Love is an emancipator of your inner and higher self.

The real you is not what you see in a mirror nor the label people place on you. You are that I am consciousness that is deeper and perfected in divine love.

There is absolutely no credible or justifiable reason to hate someone. Even those you may think are loveless or unlovable. Everyone deserves to be loved and your higher self enables you to love any- and everyone.

During Jesus' human experience on earth, there is no account of him casting blame on anyone. He demonstrated unconditional love and was the manifestation of truth. He said to those who do evil acts and who falsely accused him: "Father forgive them for they know not what they have done". Can you ask forgiveness for those who deprive you of equal human rights?

Forgive them for not finding their infinite identity and for therefore failing themselves. Loving them is excelling in your own freedom. It is hard for some individuals to evoke the divinity that God breathed into them as they are consumed by their humanity. Some of those individuals were among Jesus the God-man but they did not fully grasp His divinity. Some are still devaluing people through ethnic bias and colorism; they have not grasped the divinity of man and the sacredness of every human being.

I am going to get very personal now; I was married to my late wife, Vivette, for over 34 years but I did not fully comprehend her divinity. I don't think this is a sign of weakness because no human can fully fathom God I admired her uprightness. Often, I would say to her in all sincerity, "you are like a perfect woman." Another phrase I would use to describe her was "annoyingly caring". The flame of love for her loved ones and neighbors alike was burning incessantly. Her other-oriented nature was never swayed by what others did or say. She would still love them from a far without anger and resentment. The only weapon she would draw against those who would trouble her was the silent weapon of prayer.

I cannot recall at any time in the 34-plus years I knew her where she displayed any anger or hatred towards anybody. She was lied on and falsely accused by others. She was deeply devastated by those accusations but no anger or resentment would come out of her. She had a passion for truth. She believes in truth; one of her favorite quotes was "Hurting someone with the truth is better than making them happy with a lie."

In her time of devastation, I would constantly encourage her and remind her of the words of Jesus in the Gospel, "Blessed is ye, when men revile you and persecute you, rejoice and be exceedingly glad, because great is your reward." Those were some of her worse days., Not even her illness impacted her as much as those character assassinations.

The last 16 years of the 34-plus years of marriage, she struggled with bouts of illnesses. Nevertheless, there always existed this silent magnetism of love for God while undergoing those experiences. When the sickness would invade her mind and human body, she sometimes would be misunderstood because of the psychotic effects it had on her.

She had a heart bent on loving God and her neighbors throughout her life until she was exalted to her eternal destiny. Love is an internal divine contract straight from your eternal Source. Love was what was in her and it effortlessly came out of her in the ways she dealt with others.

I have failed so many times to demystify her illness. On the other hand, I have learned so many things about life and the human experience, especially in the last 16 years. I literally became angry with the God in me that I became speechless many times during times of agony and reflection. I cried out in silence on many occasions, saying "she does not deserve what was happening to her". There were times when I cried out in my agonizing silence and said "God, give the illness to me, I can handle it." I always thought I was tougher than her.

I lived with her for thirty-four years, seven months, and seven days out of the fifty-six years and eleven months she was living in human form on this here planet earth. I left her in bed at 6:00 am the morning of September 10, 2017. I received a call from home at some point later demanding that I rush home immediately. I had no clue that I would eventually be greeted by strangers before ultimately seeing the lifeless body of my late wife lying in our shared bedroom.

During her whole life with me I observed her manifesting her divinity, yet, I did not profoundly understand it. She embraced her divine being and this was clearly demonstrated by how she lived her life. The divine characteristics I saw her display over the thirty-four plus years of living together was a product of who she was by nature, and the religion she subscribed to.

People told lies on Vivette on occasion but she never let their unwarranted comments phase her; she knew the truth of her being. Some of those who told lies on her eventually apologized but even before they expressed their regret she had already forgive them. She did not cease to love them unconditionally without a trace of resentment. Her September 10, 2017 departure from her human body throws me into deep reflection. It sends deep signals to my inner being that I need to spend more time thinking about my own life. It added tremendous strength and insight that became a divine strength finder for me. I have learned that her physical human body is gone but the love that she represented lives on.

Based on this unique position thrusted upon me I evaluate my combination of being human and divine. In solitude and silence, I reflected on the quality of life she lived. She could not help but share the treasure of her heart and being with those she crossed paths with. The deep and selfless love she had for her God and her family was a sight to behold. The intimacy she shared with her divine source was rare. The unquenchable and unstoppable faith she had in God was just extraordinary. The death of a loved one, in my experience, is an incomparably impactful reality but I have learned that in every trial there is a divine intelligence that can be contacted through silence, or what some call 'meditation'. In my sojourn through this loss in many cases it was a time of excogitation as if I was conversating with love in another realm.

Through those silent reflections where God speaks to me in His unique way, I listened with an open heart and divine transfixion. Through divine inspiration I had a moment of intuitive insight. I still cannot demystify the fullness of it but I have discovered that enveloped in the human tent is a divine energy and consciousness that transcends the human flesh.

She fought her battle without one iota of complaint, anger or resentment. Her constant courage throughout her struggle would lead her to say; "Job was a perfect man and he lost everything and suffered." Sometimes my frustration would lead me to respond by saying, "but you are not Job."

I recalled a conversation my late wife and I had at the dining table, while we were living in Brampton, Ontario Canada. She had just recovered from an epileptic episode. She looked at me with great concern and care while displaying profound emotions,. and said in her usual soft tone, "Wallie I know it must be hard for you, and I am not able to help you". Her words and her tone triggered deep empathetic emotions. Even while facing her own deepest struggles, she was thinking of my well-being. That moment was a display of her other-oriented nature. She was this classic kind of human being who was living out her divinity.

Her life was lived with an effortless concern for others. The scarlet thread of thinking of the well-being of others was always active. She was endowed with this natural and quiet philanthropic aura flowing from her innermost being.

She had this selfless other-oriented concern for humanity. This tremendous epiphany exploded from my being, and now I can conclude with certainty that I was seeing her eternal, limitless, weightless being at work during her experience as a human.. It was the God that lived in her manifesting love. It was not the product of a mere religion, but a product of divine choice living.

Her experience and journey through that sixteen-plus years of her human struggles with illness supersedes humanity. She demonstrated a Barnabas spirit, as a wife, a mother, a sister, a friend and as the daughter of consolation. She was selfless, serene and virtuous. She was indeed like a merchant ship and a treasure hidden in the human tent.

Her humanity makes every effort to overpower her and distract her from her source/God but the absolute resiliency she demonstrates in her divinity constantly kept her faith and focus on her God. There were times she was unaware of her human self and her soul was totally caught up in her divine transcendent identity. In her own way she was saying the following words from her divine self, and in a way that is reminiscent of the words of the patriarch Job: "Although my humanity is attacked in a violent way, I will trust God in my divine being".

As I mentioned above, she had always associated her sufferings with the patriarch Job. She herself was a matriarch in her own way given her unwavering faithfulness in the face of suffering.

I watched her many times being floored and knocked out in her human flesh. However, her soul was constantly caught up in a divine domain given her tenacious faith in God. She had never lost her knowledge of the God in her. That most certainly transcends mere religious belief but enveloped in her being was this grace that was personal as she had this personal touch/connection with her divine source.

After deep consideration, contemplation and reflections, I surrender myself to the truth that love is not merely, like a magic penny that you give away and it comes back to you. Love is supreme and transcends the physical confinement of the human body. Love is a movement of your soul that marched through your higher self. It cannot be restrained or contained by human dilemma or distractions.

Love is the vibration of one's spiritual state that allows you to be completely cognizant of your divinity. It spontaneously radiates from your higher self and inner being. This experience drives your inspirational and transformational attitude. It literally ignites the light of consciousness within you; a consciousness that is separate and apart from your physical. It brings you to embrace and focus so as to operate from your higher self as an extension of God.

I could not see that invisible, limitless, and weightless being that was observing Vivette in that long period of battle with illness. She was in touch with her source I could not understand completely using my human evaluating abilities. But based on my human observation I saw her rooted and grounded in her God. The flames of unconditional love were radiating with brightness. The curtain of falsehood was torn down for her divine love to radiate.

Whenever she left her human body, it raised my consciousness and ultimately pushed me into deep reflection. I could not see that divine resolve in her; I just could not demystify her life as she displayed these coveted and admirable characteristics. Her sole focus was to overcome her adversity by adhering to divine leadership.

I saw love and unwavering trust constantly and consistently manifesting from her divine being. I was totally unaware of the divine consciousness that she was experiencing and the immeasurable depth and display of gratitude and grace that was generated by selflessness and service in love.

During a period of silent and serene reflection after her passing, this epiphany burst from my inner being. Although her humanity was shaken with the enemy of illness, her divine resolve was unwavering. She was already dead to ego in her lifetime, with her mind centered on her higher being.

Twelve days before her 57th birthday she departed; she lay down the robe of humanity. She was transferred from her human body to her permanent divine spirit. Two days before that fateful day she stated empathetically to our younger son and myself, that she "applied for a job in heaven." The statement was incomprehensible to our human senses, so we took it as one of her dramatic outbursts. Her profound pronouncement transcended our human comprehension.

On August 31, 2017, she wrote in her notebook, "God will never take something from you without the intention of replacing it with something better."

This sad departure brought much pain and loss to so many family members and loved ones. However, hopes are not shattered because her life of love is permanently engrained in our hearts. There is a silent and perpetual magnetism of love that allows no place for negative anger even during periods of great turmoil.

The unexpected passing from her human body punched me into a realm of deep reflection. I was battered for many days, weeks and months. The enlightened conclusion was that she was a divine icon with an eternal weightless and limitless soul.

I was further enlightened and came to embrace this truth that you are more divine being, than human being. You transcend the compartment and constraint of the human tent that contains who you truly are. The body is a temporary house for the higher self.

It raised me to a divine consciousness that the only perfection in this fast-moving world is the divinity of every human being. There is where perfection and permanence exist in the profound unchanging, infinite inner being that dwells within all humanity. Where divine love is the only transformational transport to the state of bliss.

The key takeaway is that that humankind should embrace love over ego accept our divine self because that is the only permanence we have. I was thoroughly inspired to share this awakening of a higher realm of consciousness. You can find the legacy of peace whilst deep in those moments of hurt, pain and loss.

Should anger be a tool utilized following the loss of those you love and cherish? Anger is wasted emotions unless it gives birth to positive change. Anger in love is how we fight our battles to win at times but it must be "righteous anger". For example, the kind of anger that is employed when people march for equality and racial justice.

It has now become clear to me that suffering is an experience that allows me to find my true self. It brings me to a place of wonderment and a profound place of awe, admiration and respect for my true identity as an extension of God.

Vivette's human departure caused the network of my mind to roam and an increase in my divine understanding to learning the conscious divinity of humanity. The purpose of your life is to have joy and fulfill happiness in your higher self. You are to have deep love for you and for others unconditionally with the deep consciousness that God lives within humanity.

Vivette gave up her human achievement and history and records her divine history in her life, as God's treasure in earthen vessels. In the mold of her religious history she supersedes religion. She was probably unaware of that implicit transformation that she made. She was experiencing things that was beyond human comprehension and was owed to the supernatural and limitless energy that exists within her divine being.

All I could render was love throughout this human attack she experienced. However, I was simultaneously inspired by her resilience in dealing with her human suffering. Love transcends all things and is able to understand and empathize with human pain in the way God does. Human intelligence cannot completely comprehend the personal struggles of the beloved.

All I could render in those moments of my human helplessness was to surrender to loving her throughout her human journey punctuated with sufferings. It became clearer in my moments of reflection of her life as a divine iconic being that her resilient faith transcends her humanity. In her life time she leaves us a legacy and trophy of indelible love.

The weapon of illness could not wear her down nor dismantle the divine connection with the God inside of her. Her resolved faith endowed her with the divine consciousness to carry on in hope. There was an eternal clarity concealed in that human tent that numbed the pain of sickness.

Paul notes the following in the New Testament; "for me to live is God and I will die with that inner resolve to Love God...I am a debtor not to the flesh but to God and not to my humanity".

While searching for answers and contemplating that she is gone too soon I was catapulted to the divine aspect of my being. I was deeply inspired with great intensity to distance myself from pain and loss and reinvent myself into someone who works from my higher self. There were no human-based explanations for the kind of pain and void I was experiencing, nor were there any man-made prescriptions available to remedy the discomfort. Losing a loved one places the grievers in a unique and strange place. It is incomparable to similar loss suffered by others because each individual would have had a unique relationship with the deceased.

In the New Testament it states; "love bears all things; love endures all things, believe all things." To briefly quote Vivette, "Don't cry over the past, it's gone. Don't stress about the future it hasn't arrived. Live in the present and make it beautiful."

As King Solomon puts it in the biblical injunction, there is a brevity to life. "The whole duty of humanity is to love God and keep His authoritative order." There is no permanence outside of your divinity that exists as the very image of God.

All things are for your divine favor. Consequently, we should give thanks in all things and draw from the divine intelligence. I saw my late wife literally loving her enemies and I have listened to her many prayers for those who despising used her and persecuted her.

She embraced her faith and manifested her divinity with reverence and tremendous gratitude to her God. It spoke to the fact that we can live in this universe while operating from our higher self. There is a perpetual flow of God empowering our lives. We must give prominence to divine endowment and experience the joy of living without fear and with a tendency towards forgiveness .

ACTIVE FORGIVENESS

Forgiving is the active vehicle to give love in a world where hate, anger and prejudice are prevalent. It permeates and surpasses human motivations and breathe a profound energy of unconditional love. This is the denying of the human and the advancing of divine awareness, allowing you to surrender to peace. By this measured swing you task yourself with the redemption of a broken humanity, to enable the divine to flow through the universe.

For God so love the world that he gave who he is through his only son. He gave himself through human flesh. It is absolutely important that we know from our higher self what Jesus shared with us: "I am the vine and you all are the branches"; the vine and branches are of the same tree; they cannot be different. We have the same possibilities to produce the same fruit of love and selflessness. God the vine is in us and allows us access to the God branch; the divine branch that produces divine fruits of love, which is the underpinning of all relationships.

We are not separate from God. We are a part of the divine source. We are connected to the divine God and the divine God is connected to us. Jesus stated empathetically: "I and the Father are One."

Therefore, we are endowed with that selfless divine nature to be able to love the world unconditionally. Do not be preoccupied with your humanity. Look deeper in your higher self where the ocean of forgiveness lies and is connected to a profound divine source. It produced overwhelming joy when true forgiveness in that deep silent outworking of the soul.

This transformational grace heals and enlightens your relationships and allows effortless love for your neighbor. Forgiveness will shift your life to a divine redemptive gear. It is truly the essential unfolding of the divine God in you, who will never leave you even if you spread your bed in hell. Forgiveness is the consciousness in knowing that the human nature is fragile and temporary. It empowers you to manifest the transformational possibilities that are deep inside your being. You are a divine being!!

We are worthy to be one with God, to know this divine truth is not blasphemous. There is a divine perfection in all of us. This perfection is the inner soul that enables you to love God with all your heart, all your soul and all your strength, and to love your neighbor as yourself. The only thing that can fully manifest true forgiveness is Love.

We are brainwashed to be enslaved with imposing rules and regulations that try to twist our hands to set up a morality forgiveness. That is a human approach trying to fulfill a divine exercise. Forgiveness is not an ego effort; it is a true enlightenment of a full surrender to your divine self.

The Great Apostle Paul in his humanity/ego goes to authorities with the intensity of purpose to shut down churches in his time in the name of rules and regulations and religion. The divine God is not about rules and regulations and religion or religious labels. His way of love transcends human rules and political correctness but divine commitment to love unconditionally.

Paul had a divine encounter with the divine Source in the invisible realm and it redirected his energy and frequency to achieve spiritual results. His experience and divine encounter spark a spiritual awakening in his life. He was transformed and became this prolific inspired author moved by the Holy Spirit and wrote several of the New Testament letters. He himself wrote "Walk in the Spirit and you will not fulfill the fleshly desire". Jesus the Emanuel was able to say through love, "father forgive the enemies because they acted out of ignorance."

This book is an attempt to take conscious evaluation and open the door on your inside to change your motivation to divine pursuit. Paul was able to operate outside of his humanity to complete God's divine task through his divinity. He states in Romans 12, "I urge you brothers and sisters, in view of God's mercy, offer your bodies as living sacrifices, holy and acceptable to God;" this is your spiritual service. Do not be conformed to your humanity – "be transformed by the renewing of your mind."

Your mind is like a battleground that requires divine strategies that cannot be crafted by the human senses. The surrendering of your soul in meekness and in the omnipotence of God is solely a divine initiative. Jesus said in Matthew – "Blessed are the meek for they shall inherit the earth." To be meek is scoffed at by many in societies because they see meekness as weakness. Meekness is the greatest strength you can exhibit; it is a selfless approach to bring clarity of your divine soul. Meekness is a silent love stream that acts as a gentle energy radiating from your heart, where the human head is no more in charge. It is not self-pronouncing and commanding but empathetic, compassionate and gentle.

Jesus demonstrates meekness in his human experience because he was manifesting His divinity over his humanity. He has all the power in the world yet he was meek and lowly in heart. He did not let human ego supersede who he was as God in the human flesh.

All of us in our higher self, that invisible part of your being with divine attributes can ignite a spiritual frequency in your being. By yielding to this spiritual awakening the soul engaged and fuel the capacity to display humbleness of spirit. You are a living soul from the very breathe of God, that will keep the divine you free from self-assertive pride. The surrendering of the divine being on the inside will enable you to experience that infinite source of being deep within you.

Let that mental harmonious energy flow from you into the universe in abundance for all to see the light of God illuminating the world. We are in this world as human beings but we are also divine being that can evoke the divine source of love. Therefore, we are not only of this world we are endowed with a spiritual connection that makes your heart love.

We are light to illuminate and salt to preserve this wonderful universe created by God who said all is good. Renew your mind to see the good in the universe the things we look at with intensity and focus. The things that are the distraction from the perfection of God's creation must be dethroned. Your meditation and thought process must embrace the divine you.

Look at the world and your comprehensive neighbors from your divine eyes to see the creation and the image of God in its fullness. The evil in the world are side shows. They are major distractions in attempt to blind our eyes from the tranquil beauty in the universe and in our fellowman.

Strive to surrender to the bliss of creation and the love in our hearts. God is love and He lives in all of us. When we acknowledge that truth peace and joy will blossom in our being. It does not matter what the human mind tells you. We must reach deep into the divine self and keep loving everyone unconditionally. We are mandated by love to love life as it is, it is a time span gift to share and enjoy.

Jesus spend over 33 years in human form and he lived out his divinity and love was the feature of his existence. During his humanity He made a positive difference and has been a positive reference. He loved effortlessly and seamlessly unconditionally.

God made us in his image to shine our lights to captivate and energize the universe. To demonstrate positive clarity and live your life in its fullness. Our motives and actions should be expressed through loving God and our neighbors as ourselves.

Love your neighbors as yourself they reflect how you see and feel deep inside your being. Practice one an otherness. Can we not see our neighbor and loved ones through the eyes of love? Search diligently for the soul of our neighbor. Anger, arrogance and hateful motives gives birth to turmoil and terrorism because all these traits are motivated by ego.

The energy of love can manifest into sweet fragrance of cure for anger and hate. The source of love is already inside of you just awaiting that surrender to that divine energy. Love must be your framework in all your relationship with all humanity. With constant consciousness that you are divine being operating from a spiritual endowment will transmit love effortlessly.

Release all your anxieties and animosity over to God who is always with you to guide, He/she is never not with you. Make every effort to live your life daily with God/Love at the center of your being. Every day you are awaken you must think about God because of that inescapable present source in you.

Nothing is so important that we should throw ourselves in a state of helter-skelter that will block that deep enlightening energy. There is no need to worry because that negative developed habit cannot change anything. There is a divine source energy that is in full control. Look for it deep on your inside so it can magnetize the right frequency. It is a very present help in time of trouble that will awaken your super manifesting divine spirit that transcend your humanity.

Human being will come across distress or anger in their journey of life but you must turn to your inner power to conquer. Anger must never be a part of our lives; although it seeks entrance to fuel ineffective solution. Make every effort to seek peace and pursue it.

Peace prepares you to accept the most powerful and transformational energy for life. Seek opportunities to serve others without expecting them to repay you as Jesus said in the gospel "I did not come to be served but to serve". Let service be your inspiration and your aspiration because loving service is the highest divine prestige.

Service is a supreme choice of life with unfathomable benefits. This commitment to service through peaceful divine consciousness will redirect anger to altruistic engagement. Give place to that gracious love deep inside you. That divine love will manifest the unconditional nature of that pure you.

This God source energy will help you to relax any feeling of anger to the transcendent feeling freedom to peaceful settlement. You are connected to the ultimate source of love that can only respond to any situation in love.

As much as possible, tell someone each day "I Love You" It is an act of your divinity. God is love – give God through your life style to your fellow man without judgement and criticism. When you are confronted with rough situations, just repeat from your soul being "I am strong" the scripture states: "Let the weak say I am strong and let the poor say I am rich" your speech and thought are very powerful.

The world occurrences are not accidents or coincidences there is an intelligent source that runs the universe. There is a cosmic coordinator that is not unaware of the events. You should strive to be filled with the untainted peace that our source left us. Peace and joy are a declaration of you will because it already exists deep in you.

Paul said in the New Testament "rejoice always", it is an antidote to victory. When your heart is filled with love daily you will have victory and live fulfilled. Live with the undeniable truth that God provide you with all things for life and Godliness. He also stated that "Godliness with contentment is full of rewards.

Take comfort in your divinity God has established you to be like Him in all manner of life. He presents Himself as Emanuel. There is that inescapable presence of God in you. Affirm in your soul that you are a divine being and that you lack nothing and no deficiency is in you. This is not a religious posture it is a divine pronouncement. God made you perfect in divinity and present you in human form to overcome all human challenges through divine thoughts.

Yourself are fearfully and wonderfully made; this undefinable fact is one that cannot be fully revealed by human intellect. Speak to your soul and remind, that quiet presence that you are always victorious. Let love for neighbors be so profound and passionate that compassionate order will be a natural phenomenon.

You are more than an overwhelming conqueror in the realm that transcend the physical limitations. Tell yourself emphatically that you are walking and living in the power of the divine God which lives in you. Let your life be that benediction of overflowing victory even outside of the conspicuous evidence. Life should not be about you and your ego but about others.

Do not get angry with society, politics and social systems that seems to be working against your belief or your likeness. Your anger and distress will never correct the ills of society but love will make the world a better place to live.

In God's supernatural domain, all things consist and He hold together the entire universe. You are positioned through divinity placed to have dominion. Our conquest will come about if we have the confidence that we have a right to be here and live as divine being although we are existing as human.

Let everyone around you benefit through your priceless legacy of peace. Manifest that bequeath treasure in the atmosphere. Walk peace, live peace, speak peace. It will energize and electrify the world. Peace operates in powerful silence in the universe feel that connection. Don't resist that divine connection let it get a hold of you to unfold the source of love without blame.

Avoid blaming and cursing those who are operating in evil ways, send them in silence unconditional love. Ask yourself what lesson I must learn from these circumstances because every circumstance should be viewed as lesson to manifest who we are.

Remind yourselves consciously that you are not engaged in a flesh and blood battle. Ask the God deep in you; how can I serve? "Emanuel said I come to serve; the apostle Paul said he is a bond slave to righteousness and a debtor not to his human self.

The implicit question is, "How can I help to rebuild the walls of society?" Use the only stray, stone wood or concrete brick you have. Embrace what you have in your hand and the divine source inside. Stop seeing yourself as apart from the source inside of you.

Refrain from saying, I don't have – instead trust in the great source to supply what you need. Live without fear because it has absolutely no value or solutions. Free your mind of fear and worry, instead instruct your mind to embrace the fact that the ultimate source/God/Love provides angels to watch over you to do your bidding.

Affirm always 'I am letting go and letting God'. Relax now and let go of the cares of life and let God be in control of your thoughts. Your thinking will enhance your life to live from your higher self where there is comfort and joy.

That joy that no flesh can attain and no man can give or take away. This is not a religious call and a call to embrace religion. This is not a call to get baptize and join a church; It is a raising of who you are outside of your human ego.

Don't believe everything the ego tells you rather believe the all intelligent source inside of you. Trust the spiritual flow of thoughts that is the inspiration (in-spirit) that creates that loving consciousness that is ever present in you. Worrying will blind your "KNOWING" and knowing is the truth that there is a greater intelligence behind your infiniteness.

This is your primary nature that weightless, limitless and endless you. You are an eternal being that exist before you were formed in your mother's womb. You are connected to the true Source that will open the floodgate of divine energy and increase your ability to manifest selflessness through love.

As God states that he has given you everything for life and Godliness – you are a divine being, therefore Godliness is your plumb line. You have influence and energy that expand bandwidth and vibration of truth in your divinity. It is undiluted, unquenchable and hunger for the taste of God's love. Let your soul be subject to its eternal and unseen possibilities manifesting your divine existence though living in a human body.

Hurricanes, storms and other disasters could be that your prayer is heard, with a divine intelligence to it. Feed your spirit with words like "He who keeps Israel will never slumber nor sleep!" Stop fighting yourself to be right strive to be kind, don't expect everyone to agree with you. Different people have other views that may not fall in sync with yours.

Be meek and tender hearted with loving one another. We all have this desire to win but start accepting other people's point of view. Never let life be about winning an argument or getting man's approval. Even if others do not agree with you be steadfast in love and loving service.

The greatest power is manifest in meekness that comes from deep inner peace. You will find power through peace and not through striving to be right or to win the debate of life. Choosing power through meekness is evoked from deep within your higher self.

When peace becomes your operational frequency, it will become effortless. Meekness and peace kissed each other. It comes from deep divine inner relaxing of your ego. It is a surrendering of your humanity and give autonomy to your divine self. It promotes super enlightenments for life's most rocky journeys, like for example losing your loved ones and other painful encounters.

Develop that inner place in your divine nature that will no longer curse the darkness and gloom of societies. That flame of enlightenment will be burning in you. This is the time when the candle of victory and clarity of the silent voice of God will calm storms of life.

God is in the midst of every circumstances – "be still and know that I am God". The I Am that I Am! Is ever present. Your political persuasion and your religious learning futile without the power of the I Am. This is when the love of God will constrain you to inner solutions.

Remember God name is love and He works through love. He redeems the entire humanity with love and through loving action. Appreciate your divinity by being grateful for who you are in human tent. You cannot be non-divine because you are made in the image of God.

God breathe himself in you so that you become a living soul and He knew you before you were formed in your mother's womb. That truth cannot be overstated it is the testament of your being. It is the perfection of your eternal existence.

Do not add or subtract from who you are, you are divine being, living in a human tent. That tent will become decrepit and disintegrate overtime. There is no need for you to be sorry for yourself. That decay is a transition to complete permanence. You are in partnership with God the divine who is your absolute source.

You are a divine being in a human house call flesh. It cannot be otherwise it is God's truth from His own omniscience. Your divine nature transcends your temporary human nature.

We must be open to evoke and explore the divine presence that flows through our being. The exploration within yourself may seems futile in the beginning. The human mind can be a major distraction from your transformation and inspiration. There must be the willingness to look silently and patiently deep within.

To reach that surrender to divine consciousness we must reach that place inside to lose the tight hold on life and let freedom reign through our being. Rest from your labor of ego and let your spirit thought reverence to the divine image surrender to divinity.

Can your living be a wholesome spiritual experience? Not to be out of touch with reality but to mount up into the realms of who you are. You are more divine than human, clearly stated in the New Testament by Jesus, "I and the father are one" (John 10:30.......Change the way you think of you and live from your higher self.

Live and work out of your divine nature to fulfill your God given purpose while you occupy this universe. Free yourselves from the past and project your future as you enjoy your present. The present is the most valuable asset that you have to build your lives.

Dignify your divinity and do not be a debtor to your flesh strive with every energy in you to love. When love is the theme of your life, you will enjoy the present. Have no fear of the future and relinquish the past.

When you transform your thoughts and control you thinking from impulse into divine inner source, you will discover peace and a place of sacred refuge. This refuge center connects us to the divine purpose, protection and security even in challenging times in life. You are held together in deep loving connection, to source. Peace and harmony become your ultimate goal.

Paul states in Philippians 3:12 "Not that I have already attained all or is now perfect, but I follow to take hold of what Christ took hold of for me". One thing I do, forgetting the past and strive towards what is ahead, I press towards the prize which God has called me heaven-ward.

Try to excel in your divine place take comfort living in the God esteemed position of divinity. Stop living on the good old days, each new day comes with new opportunities just live above your human limitations and enjoy God's gift of a brand-new day.

Now is the best day of your life; enjoy now it will past and never return. It is your gift from God, put all your divine energy and soul into the present. Have no regrets about what unfold in the past. The present is God gift to enjoy the now. Now is a constant but not a place to dwell because of its impermanence.

The Israelites were dwelling on the past carrying around it, in their heads and what they were used to. It took them 40 years to reach the promised land maybe because of their preoccupation with the past.

Do not let your journey be tiring by losing focus on the divine promise of God who is with you always. Square your shoulders and affirm "I am divine and I am that I am. Always reaffirm with super confidence, that your goal is to answer the supreme divine calling of God. Take your eyes off the human distraction of the mind and engage in pure thinking, lovely and honest thoughts.

Thoughts and ideas are the creator of every new inventions. Set your divine frequency signal and broadcast love/God on your voyage in this universe. Make no excuse to return to your old ways for no reason, whatever is done is done. You are already victorious and advancing to a higher level through your higher self. Operating from your inside, keeping that door of love open to the world.

Remove blame out of your life neither blaming others nor yourself. Do not blame your Leaders as the Israelites did to Moses there is no political solutions to the world conflicts and tragedies. Do not blame church Leaders; Political Leaders Community Leaders; not your Parents, Children, Spouse or Friend. Set your eyes on the prize and leave no room for offense and accusations.

You have that solution inside of you just be inspired. Jesus said "Blessed are you when humanity revile you, persecute and say all manner of evil about you. Rejoice and be exceedingly glad because great is your reward now and for eternity".

Think about every person who have harmed you or tried to harm you and find a way to show them love. Pray for them and send divine love in their lives. Love your enemies, it is possible through your divinity. God instructs you as a divine being, to love unconditionally. It is impossible for the human nature to love their enemies but in your divine soul all things are possible.

Live in a divine atmosphere in a world of human ego. Envy and strife, in all of these things see the wonderful and magnificent beauty of God's creation.

Never allow your religious and social distractions to throw you off course. Live in your divine frequency and maintain a clear signal of love. Jesus said in the gospel my mission is to serve all people not for men to serve me.

He made the point to highlight the fact that He is not in this temporary human experience to protect His status or reputation. I am on a divine assignment. I am inspired (in-spirit) to fulfill my divine God given mandate to set the captive free, give sight to the blind and liberate all humanity. To energized them to a divine consciousness and the recognition of all human being with God living in them.

Even if they don't wear your religious label there is a divine mandate it all human being. The religious label you carry will not affect transformation. It is the inner surrender to the divine consciousness.

Paul said 'walk in your divinity and you will not fulfill your human ego. Your divinity is the only energy that can accomplish true ambassadorship. You are here on a divine mission and endowed with divine abilities. Your ego will keep you in a constant state of fear of recognizing who you are.

It's all about knowing yourself from your source. The divine God is in you and all humanity in every generation. That fact speaks to your divine unseen, weightless, and limitless being. Be not fearful of what men can do to you. God said, "Fear not I will be with you to the end of the age". He is saying, he will be with you in everything and in all circumstances.

Never overlook or underestimate your divinity that is what keep you connected to your source who is God and God is Love. Proverbs 2 states "He will guard the course of the just and protects the way of his faithful ones; then you will understand what is right and just and fair; every good path for wisdom will enter your heart and knowledge will be pleasant to your soul".

THE HIGHEST SERVICE

G iven, that God came in flesh in the person of Jesus with a mission to serve humanity. Would you consider it a given that you were provides with mentor in human form who is supernatural and instinctively divine to follow? He said "I must be about my father's business". "I come to do the work of him who sent me". Service to God is service to mankind. Is it practical for us to live our lives as service to others?

We are equipped with divinity to serve even those who are difficult to serve. Part of the conversation that we engage in daily is the identity of synchronization and identity management. What is the measuring stick should one use to identify who she/he is?

The biological man believe that social prestige is based on their financial gain and status quo. Many fail to accept that image that look back at them in the mirror. Frist accept the unseen spirit in you that observe the real soul of the image in the mirror. When you accept that observer then you will be enabled to say to the image in the mirror "I love you". See yourselves as love wrapped up in a human frame with tremendous divine possibilities.

Jesus set us a fantastic example when he came in flesh but accentuate his divinity over his humanity. He did not focus on His humanity though

He was in human body. We all can accomplish the same results as Jesus. It is a thought process it is a thinking matter to make that valuable shift to focus on your divine self. It is a matter of the heart, soul and mind and strength facilitated by God, who is Love and is Good and made all things and all of us good.

When Moses was given his assignment to address the children of Israel, Moses had the same identity crisis or identity separation. Consequently, he asked 'who should I tell them send me'. God said 'tell them I Am that I Am". Moses was told to stand and speak in the place of the divine God – I Am that I Am. God told Moses I Am sending you as a God to Pharaoh. In Exodus 7:1 God said to Moses; "See I have made you as God to Pharaoh".

Let us transform ourselves from the religion of denominational separation or by social, cultural and economic structure. Go in your divine name "I AM THAT I AM" that is the name of God. You are endowed and empowered with the same authority as Jesus Christ of Nazareth when he walked in his humanity. He even told us that we shall do greater works than what he accomplished in His time living in humanity.

Paul said in Roman 12 – "Be transformed by the renewing of your mind". Paul was saying start thinking outside of your human limitations and be inspired, with new vision and ideas and break new frontiers.

Get out of the boundary of your humanity; find that divine place by thinking who you truly are. In Thessalonian he highlighted the fact that this human flesh is not the real you. "This robe of flesh will drop, your divine/eternal self will take a hold of the prize. In Philippians again he said "forget about this deteriorating tent; take a hold of who you are; your divinity – 'press towards the mark of your high/ divine calling".

Shift your mind; your thinking, you are partakers and a possessor of divine nature. To grow in divinity, you need to keep wholesome thoughts of your being. Not having self-pity instead be the number one you are created to be. There are two forces that lives inside of us – ego and soul. Do not feed your ego, it is not worth feeding because it will allow you not to live in your divinity. Paul said we are to die daily to self and humanity and keep ego on a low.

It is exciting and enormously satisfying to operate in your divinity because you are operating outside of your human boundary. Your soul is actively engaged in divine manifestation of your higher self. That kind of operating frequency will bring joy, peace and love to your true existence. Saint Paul instruction "rejoice evermore; and again rejoice". Full joy is wrapped up in divinity.

Let your living be divine it is the same as "walk in the spirit that you will not fulfill the desires of the flesh". For us to die to ego is to gain more divine room in your inner court because spirit operate in silence from our inner and higher self.

Ego is this human behavior that demonstrates exaggerated self-importance or think that you are more important than others. Eradicate ego from your life, it is in opposition to loving God with all your heart; all your strength; all your mind and your neighbor as yourself. Chase ego out of your business and let service to humanity be your motivation.

God selflessly demonstrated love for humanity unconditionally and came to live among us as Emanuel. God is love, God is life and God is our source who made us in His likeness. How do one replicate that extension of God who we all are? How do you produce fruit from the source? God created everything and said it is good. Therefore, if it is not good, it is not made by God, even in our human breaches there is profound good. With tremendous climate change and stratospheric dynamics, the universe exists in its perfection.

Every challenge/problem that confronts us is a distraction that we can conquer by being aware of our divine potential. When we go to God, we ought to leave our ego and surrender to the divine encounter with God. The priest of old were the ones who go into the Holy of Holies to present gifts for atonement. Now we have full access to boldly go to God who is ever present within us. The priests were symbolic of us who can now open the Holy of Holies on your inside without fear of being struck down.

We need to release our divine self to go to the source for help and answers. We must give thanks to our source and creator that we are living in a good world, home, community and country. To shift to a mindset to fulfill the divine realities in us must be an acknowledgement of our divine extension.

We are people of God with divine opportunities and possibilities. We have over seven billion people in this vast universe. Ask yourself the question: "Am I living in an angry and wicked universe?" Your answer should be "no". Majority of the people in this world are not wicked or angry. Let us characterize our world as a world of peace, goodness and God-ness, because God holds all things together. I am not saying that this world is not overwhelmed by anger, hatred, hostility and increasing terrorism.

The question is whether we will accept these minor infractions as the norm. These negative traits are distractions to intimidate humankind and sway us towards underestimating the power of God. These things are all a part of God's divine plan.

You can see the perfection of this vast universe and its glorious stratospheric diversity that operates effortlessly. The peace and comfort of nature blesses all of humanity daily by offering sunshine, snow, wind and rain.

You see the power and presence of the source in the silence of the leaves, the tree trunk, the sunlight that peeps through distinct branches. It brings tremendous peace and satisfaction to your soul. It makes your heart speak out and express just how grateful you are for life and its divine provisions. Live and appreciate creation in the fullness of its architectural design. Walk on the grass! Sit on the sand! Watch the silent stillness of the waters. These are all therapeutic activities.

We are divine beings with divine intentions and divine attributes that promote meekness, kindness, love, peace and the very presence of God. Let us live like Jesus did; in St. John 17 at His readiness to be glorified and to return to His total divinity. In verse 2, He said "You have given me power over all flesh."– "Father I have revealed your love to those whom you gave me." Jesus continues in verse 13, "I am coming to you now but I say these things while I am living in this earthly house so that they may have the full divine measure of my joy within them."

It is a fundamental truth that you must surrender your humanity to the source. Only through a full surrender of your humanity can you embrace and activate your divinity. Just be completely open and available to your creator, the ultimate source of life and sustainer of the universe. His inner existence will fill you when you make that inner authentic opening of the door on the inside to surrender to your God source.

The will to commit oneself authentically is an indication that you are not fearful of giving yourself to the divine paradigm shift. You want to liberate yourself from the constraint of the ego and take divine action. Your living is encompassed in the divine. You cannot go wrong by choosing to surrender to your inner divine being. Something better and bigger than your human self is always guiding you towards being open to the essence of your existence.

This is more than a call to perform some kind of religious, human-centric surrender. It is a call to your higher self to actively partner with God the creator. It is the embracing of the divine that is implanted in your soul and cannot be separated from your true identity. It is a resolute surrender to love unconditionally.

I can remember times when my late wife would lose human consciousness. She would say phrases such as, "I have a good thing going." She would also have a particular look on her face; the look would suggest that her spiritual essence was piercing through the atmosphere. My current evaluation leads me to conclude that she was having a transcendental moment.

As I now reflect on my time living with her in the same house, it becomes clear that there was this loving intelligence guiding her actions; even during in her time of severe illness.

There were these indefinable periods when she would sit in silence and if I entered her space, she would signal for me to be silent. It was like she was in this deep state of excogitation that required profound silence. It was a penetrable, divine experience. To this moment it is this in-demystification of experience that transcend her humanity. She had this unstoppable, unshakable desire to serve God and humanity.

You can penetrate and influence the world through loving service to mankind. Jesus effectively proved this to be true. He prepared us to serve humanity through our divinity and encouraged us to shy away from self-promotion.

Through meekness and peaceful conversations with God you can develop this indomitable spirit.

Complete surrender to meekness, gentleness and peacefulness will evoke a universal energy to a spiritual path. There is an infinite power in your innermost being that will reveal a bigger spiritual plan for the journey of life. To experience more love streaming through your being must reach the place of passionate surrender to divinity.

Do not be imprisoned by your circumstances. The way you handle challenges and sufferings is by finding the divine opportunity in the process. Your mind is extensively more powerful than your circumstances, no matter how dismal it may look to your human eyes. The breath that you breathe has divine originality and it is taking you to divine opportunity.

FREEDOM FROM WITHIN

T he human being has a divine freedom that can stream from the inside. That divine extension of God can enhance your total freedom. Do not be imprisoned by your circumstances – your mind is inexhaustible and unstoppable. It is carving and creating tools for life through loving freedom. Your mind power is greater than your circumstances. The path is already smoothly laid out for you. Your day of liberation already exists within you.

Always affirm deep in your soul that all is well. Just put your confidence in the future as you enjoy the present. Be joyful in these times and evaluate your spiritual potential to make great accomplishments through the expression of freedom.

Whatever is the nature of the situation there is a divine solution on your inside. Life is unfolding by God's design and errors can never be associated with the divine source. Take a look at nature and see it unfolding. God in His glory and His untiring labour for your good is a tremendous part of your freedom. God lives in you and you cannot exist otherwise. Whatever presents itself to you as wrong is immediately detected by your higher self.

The human judgment and false imagination can conceal that freedom. Your present situation and frightening experience received with radiant love is the escape route to full freedom. Develop the divine consciousness to listen to God speaking in silence in the midst of your turmoil.

The God in you is a girding and guiding your mind to the divine power in you. Let go of any distraction as to how your desired result will be accomplished; it's a divine task filled with divine silence and enlightenment. You have the light of God in you that will illuminate the dark alleys in your life journey and lead you away from the emotional precipice. There is a divine power in you that can pull that light out of your being and shine through any situation.

Your innermost being, which is your soul, is able to empower you to create a path to your promised land. God dwells inside your being, offering constant reminders that he is present and engaged. It is very easy for the outsider to criticize you but you are the keeper of the insider of your own choices.

Choose the eternal path to peace and bliss. Your soul always has a higher plan for you. Be determined to live as the divine version of yourself. It is a decision of your willpower to achieve your goal of peace and freedom. There is true freedom even in your human incarceration.

Determination is a way of exonerating yourself from the prison of fear. It can also move you to a place of favour. It will acquit you from the prison of poverty and control into the freedom of abundant life.

In the New Testament Jesus said 'All that is mine is thine'. Determination will drive new frequency to your mind and destroy thoughts of limitations. Like an athlete, you are training to achieve your highest goal. This training gives birth to inspiration (in-spirit), and will allow your inner self to get a hold of your divine capabilities.

If you are imprisoned by poverty, you must post your own bail bond and release yourself with a decisive spirit to first change that thought process. You are endowed with divine thought to transform your social mindset and liberate yourself from any false label.

Reach deep inside of yourself for that divine connection as it is the one and only liberator you have. Your circumstantial imprisonment needs that inner love, peace and joy, that is the gift of life. That shift will create from your thoughts, the energy flowing from the inner self, allowing for complete freedom in an inspirational domain. As I stated before, there are no human solutions to any problem. You must reach deep into your inner self where the solutions to your life problems lie.

When you wake up each day, it brings new opportunities. Look for those changes that each new day brings. Opportunities never cease to exist because God creates a perfect universe and states that all is good. Look for it by accessing that divine consciousness on the inside to experience a realm beyond the physical.

Whatever our experiences are, they have deeper purposes for its manifestation. Human physical self cannot attain the profound joy of divine actualization. If you look on the outside, you will stumble and fall into another ditch of humanity. It can be very dark on the outside where you can only operate from your human physical self. There is a light within that soul, an energy in you that is shining on new meanings and allowing for tremendous enlightenment.

Experiences of life can captivate you and lead to contemplative challenges to your experience as a human . The undeniable truth is that you have a love connection straight from a divine source that is assisting you to see the way. Love is the divine gift from which a human being can come to the realization of this simple truth; the truth that you are inseparable from your divine source. It is virtually impossible to use the human mind to comprehend the other person, except through love.

Through love you are able to connect with your beloved traits and personality in spite of its flaws and damages. There is this inseparable connectivity that can only be deciphered in the sphere of the spiritual. This spirituality supersedes your religion and religious label.

Authentic and profound satisfaction in your life experience is realized when you unfold that intrinsic truth that you are always connected to the divine source of love. The infinite creator manifests through you when you develop that energy of selflessness and find peace deep within. Be satisfied with yourself and be deeply relaxed in the truth that your divine connection has placed you in the safety of your destiny.

My late wife of over 34 years constantly demonstrated that her primary motivation for life was to live according to a divine plan. She never thought her faith in her source was a secondary rationalization.

She suddenly passed away two days after she emphatically and joyfully expressed to our younger son and myself: "I applied for a job in heaven." We simply laughed it off as one of her usual dramatic moments. I am now convinced that she was instinctively driven by a divine connection to her God who was ever-present in her.

I can recall that fateful afternoon when that same son, Shawn, called me and frantically ordered my hasty return to the house: "daddy you have to come home now!" The phone went dead before I could respond to him. I sensed the ultra-urgency in his voice. I was spell-bound that moment, filled with undefined curiosity. I was at work doing a twelve-hour shift. It was at the ninth hour that I received the call. My parental and husband role pierced me as I was faced with the unknown. I immediately tossed the work phone onto my co-worker's lap and hastily informed her that I had to leave At that moment, I did not care about the consequences associated with leaving prior to the end of my work shift

My curiosity and anxiety never came close to my soon painstaking discovery. Not in the slightest did I think that I would go home to find my wife lying lifeless. I was dumbfounded. I collapsed onto the floor when I discovered her lady there. The temple from which she lived out her human experience was the only thing present at that moment. Her weightless and limitless divinity was now absent.

It was the most painful experience I have ever had in my whole life. That moment of tragic discovery took a toll on my living experience.

The finality of 34 years was now unfolding the scroll of our life together. In these few moments, our entire life story was unfolding from my being to the present experience.

I recalled entering driveway seeing emergency Medical Service vehicle (EMS) In front of the building. I was still fill with a mountain of curiosity but not expecting the finality of my discovery.

I parked my truck and briskly glided to the door to find two policemen standing guard at my front door. They greeted me with a pause somberly and made the inconsolable revelation to me. This was the worst news I have ever presented with in my whole life.

The officer on my left slowly said, "Mr. Neil your wife has passed away, you may need to take a break before you go into the bed room". That was a shocker! It was like a thunder bolt hit me in my forehead! My two knees collapsed, and I fell to the floor, as stated before. I was now held up by two officers, one holding my right arm and the other holding my left. This was the arrest of my fateful discovery. It was the incarceration of my entire 34 plus years of marriage. It was the end of made together era and message of no return. It was the striking reality of "until death do us part".

It was totally devastating as I immediately felt a void in my whole being. This call I received from our younger son in that emergency and desperate tone was to cement the most interruptive news that one could ever listen to.

He called with deep emotional desperation and urgency, wounded by his own discovery and loss. He went into a temporary isolation to recover from his shock and bewilderment. I watched my two sons even today in their herculean task of picking up the pieces to move forward with this sudden unexpected exit of their mom. It struck that placed in their being that starts a deep instinctive conflict that is irremovable. I would say to my sons many times, I cannot feel what you guys are feeling, but I can only imagine because if I was just husband and the pain is so severe and she was you only mother.

Even with that desperate call that became soundless, that raised my curiosity and melts my emotion, it did not raise me to the expectation of this finality. The thought of death never enters the intersection of my mind while driving home to receive this shocking disclosure.

The fact I leave her alive at 6 am. in the morning the only thing that came close was that maybe she became sick because of her years battling with that enemy of illness. The finality of that phone call was not even thought of in the least.

When I drove in the yard and saw the EMS and police vehicles, I thought they were there to take her to the hospital. My emotional investigation still did not drive me to the destination of death.

The reality of entering my front door and saw the two officers at the doorway instilled a transfixed emotion. For months after the first indelible and grueling announcement rings in my ears. The greeting from those two policemen and the feeling of their hands holding me up became a permanent imaginary for a long time. The memories of that fateful evening dropped my heart from the original place of over 34 years of togetherness to a human emptiness that happened in a moment.

My emotional well-being was shattered in the space of two weeks I lost 15 pounds and never gain it back for well over two years. The new of death separation became an agonizing discontinuous fixture in my life. Although I was confident that she lived a good life and touched many lives, including her two sons and she fought a good fight and kept her faith. I was still paralyzed with losing her especially in that sudden unexpected way. I don't know that there is any way a person can prepare for the biological, human departure of the beloved. Your beloved becomes your motivation, inspiration and enabler for you to advance to you true potential and aid you in self-actualization.

The mourning was painful but from time to time I talk to her from my inner divine being, and she would answer me back. Each time I see her I saw her with a glowing feature in divinity.

She said to me the first I saw her and converse with her in her new reality; "Wallie - as she would to call me - I am ok and I am happy!" After her passing many times I was in the kitchen cooking and had to wipe tears from my eyes and walked away from the stove to recover myself. Those experiences were a kind oy therapy for me and the reality kicked in that we are more divine than human being. IN these moments is like she was there in the kitchen telling me how much season to put in the pot.

The divine spirit was present but the physical human was absent those times when she was in that kitchen, I would not only converse but go behind and hold her tight to my body. The memories were alive and stimulate my spirit and evoke some measure of comfort that unfold an instinctive smile. I could hear her spirit still telling me how to cook and my stern response "I will not cook like you, leave me alone, I know what to do".

I can remember one day about 6 months of her passing I was overwhelmed upon reflection. I walked from the living room to the bedroom lay down. In some miraculous way I saw a Father's Day card that she gave me on the Father's Day before her passing 2017 lying on the floor.

I picked up the card, opened and the words written in her own hand writing pierced my eyes. It reads; "Thank you for all the love, care and laughter you bring to our home and family". My heart melted with another dose of the reality of the loss of a beloved friend who demonstrated unconditional love for me. A spontaneous flow of tears warmed my cheeks, however amidst the tears and smile slowly wormed its way through my face. I found myself speaking out in audible tone, saying as if she was there with me, "you gave me the reason to"! I stretched across the bed and had almost a full replay of our lives together. The good times, the bad times and the disagreeable and makeup moments. I had laughers and tears in between that rehearsal. In this extended rehearsal of our lives, I had flash back of a December 2016 experience, as follows:

I will always dance in my home especially, she knows it and my children knows it, many times they would make a laughter of my dancing. As long as I can recall from February 1983, when we joined together as one, I have been trying to get her to dance with me but she avoided dancing. She would constantly say "I can't dance". In response to that claim I have always tell her it's not a competition, you dance to please no one just to enjoy yourself. That I still believe today.

Interestingly in December of 2016 we were at our friends' home as part of the Christmas celebrations. As usual my friend was playing music and most of us gathered there in the celebratory vibes. Everybody was enjoying themselves and some were dancing and it was super enjoyable.

She clearly got caught up in the spirit of the atmosphere and never care if she could dance or not. To my shocking awakening in the midst of all these people of faith dancing my wife calmly walked over and hold me and started dancing with me. It was so infusing and exciting I could not find my dancing feet so we awkwardly dance together for the first time for the over thirty years I have been trying to dance with her. It of course a scintillating experience that lit the room brighter with laughter and awe.

I recalled the next day we were at home and I shared it with Shawn our younger son. All three of us had a belly full of laughter of the new chapter in our lives together. It was a phenomenal episode going down memory lane of over 34 years together as a couple.

I ended by saying, "thank you for being my friend for loving me unconditionally for who I am. It was like she was present in the human physical form in the room as stated above. I was overwhelmed by this divine encounter; it was an awaken and enlightening unbelievable episode. When you leave this physical tent, your eternal being is very much alive as the extension of God.

In that heart melting moment, I was super convinced that she was present in her divine form. The eternal, weightless, limitless and infinite being that was formed before her ninety plus mother who was still alive was born was present with me to tell me she is ok.

My soul came alive and reminded me that she is present in her eternal spirit talking to me and from that day I resolved to accentuate my divinity over my humanity as Emanuel did while on earth.

It could not change my fate of the human loss but it raises my consciousness that there is a brevity to the human life but our soul is eternal. It also helped me to realize that there is a divine comforting presence that will provide the tools of courage to aid me through my painful situation and replace peace where there is pain.

I could not bring her back but my soul found favor in the memories of her grace. Losing your loved, one is not a small feat. The glorious encouragement is that beloved is away to her divine ascension and divine assignments. I have constant dialogue with her in the spirit and felt her answering me back,

she talks back to me in the invisible realm with new divine enthusiasm. I can recall one night I was in conversation with her it was so intense and real, that I almost said to her I thought you were dead. Immediately the thought came to me saying she is a divine being and is an eternal soul.

I consoled myself many times with the fact that if I had passed before her, she would have to deal with the circumstances of loss. That consolation gave me tremendous courage to move on with my life and that my life is not void of its true identity because we are all divine being living in a human being that will pass away. That experience of the passing of my beloved has driven me with intensity to accentuate my divinity over my humanity and that I am never alone even if I spread my bed in hell!

Death is only a physical departure of the beloved. The undeniable fact is that it comes with unexplainable emotional and physical pain. In my human recollection that has been the deepest experience of lost I have had. I have also learned as I mentioned in this manuscript before, that there is a divine intelligence in every tragedy and pain. Life is a divine path that surpasses the finite and finds it true existence in the divine plain of infinity. You are equipped with a divine light that can shine in any dark moments because we are all light of the world. All in this sense is not exclusive, in include every human being in the whole universe

Never affirm or dwell in the dark by saying, life is hard and time are difficult; I am lonely; I am sad and I can't make it. See yourself living in universe that is illuminated and there are great and diverse dimensions to living.

Extend your thoughts to a universe that supersede the human confinement. Engage in new thoughts that will give birth to new vision to reach your ultimate goal in excellence and excited joy. It is very possible to live in this universe with this confidence that your future is bright.

Don't live a retroactive life and let retrospective thoughts take hold of you and retard your future. Use the present as a breakthrough platform to launch a triumphant entry to the great arena of service to your fellowman.

When you read the daily news, listen to the various news cast, get updated on the different war zone. These external forces are at work through illegal drugs, guns, wars, ego craze and disregard for human lives. It is a time of tremendous challenges but with immense possibilities and unstoppable opportunities.

Although these things are happening around you away from you, the salvation of man is still alive in you through unconditionally love. Live from the inside the real opportunity of life is not lost in the past; never think the worst is yet to come, the worst is already over like a passing wind.

The divine soul will not allow you to focus on what you do not have but to draw upon the inner self to make life a supreme experience. In Moses case in the Old Testament, he had a rod and David had three stones and a sling to accomplish and defeat the battle that confronts them. What you have may not be in your hands but your mind and thoughts is an effective creator of solutions. No battle belongs to you and never meant to be fought with physical human being, it is domain of the divine resolvable strategies.

DIVINE CONFIDENCE

It is possible to conquer with divine confidence in the mist of chaos, crisis and despair. Each moment of despair assisting you to your higher self. Once you are listening to that silent voice and gentle voice of help and comfort it will cast away your fear. In that moment of deep internal awaken and divine listening you can feel indomitable.

In the New Testament Jesus said 'Happy are they that mourn, for they shall be comforted'. You are a divine being. if you succumb to your human being your immunity will be weaken and your hope and courage will be shattered. Find the answers in that treasured soul that no man can destroy nor disable, because it is eternal, weightless and invisible.

Francis of Assisi was working on the outside in his garden when he was asked the question "What would you do if you knew you were going to die today". From his divine inner-self, he answered "I would continue hoeing my garden". This is a classic example of living with confident in your divine self. It is not a mere belief rather it is the knowing that you are created in the image and likeness of God.

This confidence is far more than positivity and optimism and more than a strong hope. This kind of confident is knowledge by experience of your divinity and your eternal future. Jesus said "for that purpose I came into this world to die, I have no fear" He did not fear those that can only kill the body. Your goal and courage can give birth to fundamental change and break new frontiers in your life. Fear no criticism or changing your customs and manmade culture. Strive to know who you truly are.

This is a place of knowing God is your source of the present and the future and our life is not uncertain but very real and eternal. It is more than something handed down to you by religion. It is a firm and affirmed knowledge that you are distinguished from the lower animals as an exalted divine being.

This is a knowledge that far exceed intellectual acclaim social and scholastic achievements. It is the transformation through inspiration that reaches into our soul being. You are a unique eternal being with inner strength that equipped you to rise above any situation and live your truth of being.

INSPIRATION-
(I.E. IN-SPIRIT)

I nspiration is a divine experience that open your soul to the universal truth of your divinity. You become unstoppable in the spirit with a capacity of great creativity to life's internal solutions. Your power will not be imprisoned; your true desire and destiny will mount up with wings like eagle. To be inspired is a walk in the counsel of your divine source, that will bring about tremendous transformation (i.e. to operate outside of your humanity).

The reggae icon Bob Marley who in his inspirational outburst song, " Emancipate yourself from mental slavery, none but ourselves, can free our minds. Have no fear for atomic energy, cause none of them can stop the time". He had an inspired message for the world, that message is unstoppable and unchangeable. He got this cosmic view fill with divine truth that he was compel to share.

The source enables the proliferation of this message to go out and reinforce the divine possibilities in the human being. This inerasable truth is documented in his song. Your freedom is from deep inside your being. The path is already surfaced, the fact that you are an extension of God your maker

He was dubbed one of the sexiest men in the world in his time; one of the most transforming man and one of the most impactful creators of musical genre in his time. Clearly this is no coincident but of divine source and intent because the line of that particular song as I quoted above as well as others is a mantra for the world.

His songs are quoted in all circle of the world as a conscious stabilizer to humanity. You must find who you are by merging into your divine essence to encounter inspirational experience from inside of you. To manifest unconditional love, you must be inspired from within to abandon self-sabotaging practices that are constrained by being focused on your mere humanity. The release of inner-self, will transform your thought process to accept the fact that you are a limitless, divine and invisible being living in human form.

Inspiration draw divine wisdom and energy and empower you to make transformational changes to all humanity. It drives you to work with all that exist in your higher self. It allows you to be rescued through the divine ability to sort out who you really are as a divine being.

Inspiration properly balance immediate gratification, to a broader prolific effect of transforming peoples experience. Sorrows or sufferings will frame you with future rewards like making valuable contribution to the upliftment to the human race. It is revealed by many artistes to put their experiences in writings, songs, chanting, hip hop and other performing arts. There is a vibrational impact from these artistic births.

When you are inspired it brings out that uniqueness and emotional captivation that distinguishes you from operating in the normal human boundary. Inspiration brings transformation; as I stated before, transformation is when you operate incredibly beyond your human limitations. It not only brings unquestionable changes to the inspired but is tremendous influence and impact to others.

You can overcome inner emptiness by opening that inner door on your inside that leads to the inner court of your true self. Sometimes you can find yourself in a strange place physically, emotionally, mentally, socially and economically but you are more than all the above. In these times your creativity become inexplainable. These are doors to exit turmoil to find treasure.

It requires more than human interventions to bring stability and purpose to life. Your whole human structure can be threatened and you could start to feel a sense of indignity and your attempts seems futile. This is what is called a predicament which means, "no human way out" of your situation but there is always a divine way and solution.

THE POWER OF
CHANGE

Change entails a tremendous amount of mental and psychological adjustment. Migration is one of those change that calls for a mental re-invention and paradigm shift. It requires a fixity of purpose and a social infusion of your new environment. The reality of leaving the comfort and culture comes with anxieties, agitation and tremendous adjustment. This adjustment has to be progressively planned in the processing of settling in your new environmental realities.

I recalled when I migrated to Canada with my family, in 2006, there was a feeling of tremendous detachment and trepidation. I was experiencing a social disconnect as a new resident in a strange country. I was seeing myself as part of this enormous melting pot.

Observing the diversity of people, who are speaking different, dressing different and clearly the common factor among all the groups is, searching for socioeconomic answers. The experience put you on the track of a emotional roller-coaster. I felt like an outsider that was misplaced. Like you are in the middle of a circus where you are forced to participate in this inevitable parade.

This was a time of re-invention; and a paradigm shift. Your life moved from comfort zone in search of inspired elegance. It was like you were thrown on this huge stage for this competitive this audition.

To find your role on this stage requires and internal encounter to emerge with that suitable role. This is a time when you are called to respond with a broad and open mindedness to maneuver and manifest your skills. I mentioned earlier in the maxim, "you can be anything you want to be in life". I am sure there are many who believe that myth and lose who they are.

I have learned that that changing where you live geographically will not change who you are. I f you're are a great salesman you are great where ever you are and going to the studio don't make you into a singer. I stated in this manuscript before that the solution to any challenges or problems you are confronted with is in in you. If you perceived a solution you have to pursue that solution deep from within your inner being.

The response that is required is more than strong human confidence. Its calls for gentleness, courage, patience and inner guidance. Your whole system becomes contemplative in the presence of inevitable changes.

The desire and determination to breakthrough in any new adventure must be mustered for the battle of the change. The battle of change is a mind shift, a paradigm shift. The manifest desire and drive must be geared to your expectations of migrating in the natural and in the divine or spiritual. This desired expectation will be met with opposing cultural the conventional practices of the new country of the experience.

In my personal experience in this season of change my psychological roller coaster was extremely active. It was a time when my mind was still clinging to Jamaica where my stability was established. I felt powerless and like I was pushing against this enormous tidal wave.

I felt incapable of creating and manifesting the desires I carved out based on my research. I was now in a self-made dream with undefined interpretations; therefore, having no tools to carve out my vast vision.

Of course, finding yourself in this new reality you start searching opportunities to get settled in this now new home. The feeling of self-blame and wrong-choice starts to set in, maybe bordering on a slight depression. Amidst that vacuum or empty space on the inside you sense that greater essence deep in your heart. That silent stillness, unravelling in soft surges, saying all is well and the unfolding of things will come. You have to listen to who you are in the divine. No human can help you out of your circumstances they can only help to create the environment for that change.

On your inside you are processing rhetorical questions like; did I make a mistake? Was this a wrong decision migrating? and so on. Deeper in your innermost being far beyond the human being the answer coming back to you; not a mistake you are in step with your source. That fact is at that time I could not feel the intensity of that truth.

In my search in this new geographical and social darkness, I was introduced to a program for new Canadians. I was now socializing with different people from many different parts of the globe. Everyone clearly was manifesting some level of anxiety with one common goal to find new opportunities in this strange land.

The stories were different but certainly similar all looking to fit into their new place to call home. To find home away from home. In my years of living here in Canada peoples in their conversations will always say "back home".

We all spent three months in a classroom learning about our new beginning and hoping for our aspirations to be realized. This was an attempt to help us to get adjusted to our new environment as new Canadians.

The experience was profound, one that enlightened us to where we were. It was calming and to some extent healing of some of the anxieties. We were prepared for embracing our new country and to make the best of its opportunities.

At the end of the three months the social services did not solve all our challenges as new Canadians but helped us to allay fears and replaced it with some trust. At the end of the program I was unanimously chosen by the group to give the valedictorian speech.

The following was what I wrote and presented: -

"Ladies and gentlemen this morning we want to pause to say thanks to the executive director of Inter-Cultural Neighborhoods Social Services (ICNSS), (clearly a great visionary) her graceful staff and all the stakeholders for equipping and enabling us to go forward into the Canadian work force.

We are no longer inhibited by cultural elements that can deter us from achieving our optimum goal. The way is clear! The lights are working! The cop is gone! We can now proceed with caution. Let me pause a little longer to express special gratitude to the presenters who have displayed dedication, commitment and care as true communication experts that free people from seeing the world according to normative societal prescription.

With their proactive and provocative approaches, they have all prepared us to be possibility thinkers and proactive opportunity takers. Thank you all for facilitating and fostering an inseparable inter-cultural and integrating experience that is essential in networking. This experience you have exposed to us and exposed us to has provided student from all walks of life with tools of persuasion. You have prepared us to use the language to liberate ourselves from the confining walls and enable us to enter the circle of ready candidates for the Canadian job market.

To my fellow graduates…The traffic lights are back on! The barriers are broken! The cop is no longer standing at the intersection; we are free to proceed according to prescribed standards. We are armed with Canadian experience. This is your land. Own it! Now we know who we are; where we are going and who are these others!

Take advantage of all the tremendous opportunities and possibilities that are presented. Go forth fearlessly and "attempt great things for Canada and expect great things from Canada."

I shared this speech in my book because I want to highlight the fact that we are our own solution. God knows I was not in the frame of mind to start from scratch again but I went into an environment that redirect my mood. I had to submit selflessly without ego to the fact that my future lies deep within my Higher self as an extension of God. Others can only help to set the stage but you are the protagonist and the performer,

Another reason for sharing the speech is to engage my readers to be willing to migrate from your human comfort zone and soared to live through your divine being. To make the shift will involve a kind of re-invention of your inner self I called your higher self. It may mean you have to take a walk from the comfort of religion and transcend denominational barriers. It needs to be an implicit resolve to make the impossible, possible through love and loving service. It will feel strange and awkward but it requires a surrender to your divinity.

This strange detachment was not resolved by the Social Services and the interaction with the human bodies present. Until I entered into my inner self, into my soul – the eternal part of who I am that knows no boundary or limitations. This new reality was only my outside story in a strange place. There is remarkable power and possibilities in re-invention and revision of your true self

I was deeply aware of one thing and that is, I was not without hope because my thought process was actively engaged in search for viable outcome. I did not know exactly how my family was making the adjustment. I would encourage advise and facilitate the inevitable change process as much as I could. I knew from a human perspective that it was a tremendous challenge for them. I also knew that no change and solutions can come about outside of them.

I observed tension, anxieties and exceeding uneasiness in my beloved family.

Consequently, I became very contemplative and my expectations starts to be weakened. I remember my eldest son in a very anxious and stern tone said to me "daddy why you come here, you have everything in Jamaica and he repeat why you come here". At the time I had no real and ready answer, I paused and looked at him very quietly and thoughtfully for a moment and responded reassuringly in very low tone. "I came for you". The dynamics of life has a divine built in connection that you must allow the frequency to flow.

I could only emerge from that emotional roller-coaster and physical powerlessness when; I opened the door on my inside and look within I drew from my source. That part of you that cannot be confine by any socio-economic, psycho-social or eco-ethnical barriers will always give answers. When you connect to your divine soul that existed before you were formed in your mother's womb is always present to tell you that you are your destination. That you are always existing, as divine and eternal. There is where you will evoke a ray of light and real hope will replace fear for you and your beloved.

I gave this scenario to tell the story that where ever you are your mindset is your emancipator. Deep inside every human being is a power that is so unstoppable, it can literally connect you to the divine source that you are. This great power is guiding your life. Your decision and leaps in life has a divine force that is steering to a divine direction.

This guide force exists in all of us and once we surrender to it will lead you to find profound inner peace and joy to live imbedded in our spiritual nature.

My outer observation and social experiences had brought me to a very dark place in my history. That was the exact opposite of my green pasture expectations. I can remember my new experience in this huge melting pot, stirred with internal investigation. From the core of my being I set the frequency of willingness to listen to my higher self as to what my reality is carving out for me. My childlike curiosity raised my consciousness to answer my new awareness. It drives me to stop and define who I am and where I am, and how to get out of this internal struggle.

My thoughts went still for a moment, emerging from deep within me where all solutions exist. A song that Bob Marley song popped up from hard drive into my spirit and became my mantra: "Time will tell; think you're living in heaven but you are living in hell, time alone will tell". I did not hit the delete button because it serves as a constant reality check for a while.

When you enter into your inner court and removed the veil and overcome the intellectual drama the divine spirit takes on the role as the protagonist. You realized that you have to be engaged in more than a mental drama but a spiritual conversation with God source.

My decision to migrate to Canada was fully thought out, it was fundamentally to experience a change of environment particularly with my family in mind. When you experience the peace and calm download from your divine source, it enlightens you and serves as a signal and clarity.

Your divine consultation prepares you to have a core willingness to listen to source. That decision brought me into my infinite space which is the foundation of your existence the breath of your maker.

That predetermination became the buttress in the thunderstorm of the change. It brought more consciousness and continuous streaming on the inside to make the journeys adjustment. Even if in the human you felt like you are living in hell and the helter-skelter of socio-geographic shock invades your humanity. You know that if you spread you bed in in hell God is there.

I let go off my humanity, and deepened my divine connection to my source for divine counsel. The strength and vibration enlightened my soul teaching me a greater understanding of my present reality. This awakening ignites new energy to pull me through this heat of change. When you are released from the outer distractions and embrace that amazing divine presence and enter into who you really are you experience the infinite energy of your source.

During this connection with my divine self, in conjunction to feeling my way around to adapt to the change my late wife became extremely ill worst that I have ever seen while living in my home land Jamaica. Now it was forcefully overwhelming because I was far away from our social support groups.

She was in and out of the hospital literally every month for the first few months of living in this new country. With no social support from friends and kinsman I was forced to look deep inside of me for new resolve. I was literally drunk with emotional pain, that was hypnotizing me. Amidst this mental roller-coaster it threatened my stability and placed me in a provisional mode.

The blanket of hope was now covering short my closest friend and support was now suffering with illness. This exceptional situation was accelerating to shatter my attempt to make something of my transition to Canada. In these moments you forget that these external circumstances are the vehicle to take you to your inner spiritual source that is far beyond your humanity.

I was moving from job to home to hospital and from the hospital to another job. That became the cycle for months. The past became completely useless to me all I have to act on is my present circumstance. The jobs were physical nothing to compare to the executive positions I held before my migration.

They required physical strength to execute these tasks that was depleting my energy level. The only tireless source you have is to reach to you higher self in divinity where you are weightless and infinite.

Status quo and labels were of the past; you have to use what you have like Moses in the Old Testament, where God asked him what he has in is hand. His answer was "a rod" and God told him to use it to show His divine power.

The past always disappears and the present is always with us as the only active constant in life. The present was all I had that was my rod. This called for deep spiritual heights, was not about going to church and embracing a new religion. It was indeed a profound awakening and a productive enlightenment. I recognize it what I call in fullness that I was the Temple of the Source as the extension of God.

I was reminded of who I am; (more divine than human) this is the times you have reach to you higher self. The manifesting of the sacredness of overcoming obstacles was not an option. The human strategy was null and void. The need for the awakening and the enlightening spirit from your inner- most being was the only calming and clarifying campaigner. That divine power from inside was the only source that could effortlessly presents outcomes. My daily guide and energetic vibration guided me from within. I had to take charge to assure all is well even in turmoil. That source is where your answer became; I am well! I am wonderful! and I am happy!

Those who are aware my story of my late wife illness, always say to me; "you are a strong man" Of course they are referring to my composure to endure and withstand the inevitable challenges of my realities. My response, always; is I am not, but it is my responsibility and commitment. The fact is I had to stand with her because we both made a solemn covenant with each other. "I did not consider myself strong, it was just my responsibility and the right thing to do. I just have to confront it with a conquering spirit.

I have learned as stated before that every solution of all challenges/problems are within you. Deep inside me I knew I was being presented with a bitter cup and there was some divine intelligence in all of it. My strength was not in my humanity, but in my divinity.

I realized that I had no choice but to accept my training with the knowledge that I am a divine being. We all are divine beings living with a divine promise that our source will never leave us nor forsake us.

If you take the wings of the morning, or even spread your bed in hell that source is there. With all that divine assurance the humanity caved in with unbearable encounters but your divinity is always silently strong. Many times, it was so overwhelming that I felt angry with God/source.

I profoundly know that he is with me and not against me. I knew I was made in His image and he is my source and like the apostle Peter said in the New Testament, "I am kept by the power of God". Yet with all that knowledge I was running out of human endurance, but the perfect quietness of endurance in divinity kept me going. I have learned that being angry with God is being angry with yourself, because you are an extension of God.

This experience of hope and victory Is not prescriptive; it emerged from an unknown place within you who is limitless, weightless and eternal acknowledge your divine identity.

Deep in your soul the divine source will awakens you to a place higher and deeper than your humanity. It doesn't matter what is your socioeconomic status, background or geographic origin. In you dwells this source of unconditional love.

That implant in you is that spiritual discernment to hold and 'KNOW' without a doubt that you are more than an overwhelming conqueror. I learned to respond with open minded, divinely generated patience, meekness and kindness.

The noise and urgency of your dilemma is never the sound to respond to. The quiet silence of the divine, saying without emotions "be still and know I am God". That's the one who speaks through silence you should listen to for deep inspiration to make victory be your cheer leader.

The illuminating fact fused in me an enlightening awakening. It constructs clarity of thought that my answers were more than human thoughts and contemplation.

It was divine actions that was taking place in me during the training process. Your battle was not physical therefore it was not my role to fight it but to "be still and know". This is for all humanity who are all endowed with divinity. I realized that my cross bearing was my real asset that I must accept. Sorrowing for self is a disengagement from your source. It is judgement you pass on your strength remain in the spirit of who you are. Judgement will disable you breathing in your path to liberation in the mix of life.

I acknowledged that I have to be my main ingredient in this huge melting pot. My inability to demystify and fathom the increase illness of Vivette my late wife was frustrating. The ability to remain calm in and maintain a peaceful composure was threatened.

The admiration throughout the over sixteen years of her physical human attack was that she had a unique and resilient faith in her God. I stood with her in payer and with many tears. On the flip side, there were times I thought praying was futile and fruitless. I was side tracked by my humanization of her experience of sufferings.

Her human suffering stretched my faith, at times I thought to myself she was spiritually innocent as a baby and did not deserve it. There was no reason or need to curse or criticize or run away. I stood with her between jobs every step of the way until this sudden and painful exodus from her humanity. She departs from us in the human form, that fateful Sunday but leave her iconic mark deep on our hearts.

In all of the struggle, mentally and physically her unique task to bring transformation to many lives even in suffering, was divinely manifested. When I got impatient with God, she would always remind me of Job in the Old Testament of the bible who suffered as a perfect and upright man as the scripture stated in (Job 1:8). I watched her acknowledge it as her divine self over her humanity. She held firm to her source without one iota of complain and comprise of faith.

She leaves me with tremendous inspiration from her life; it inspired me to write this book, that "we are more divine being than human being".

As my family and I embarked on this new journey of living Canada, leaving our kinsmen, relatives, friends and culture my eyes literally became darkened with the stress that came on my physical biological self.

I remember one incident that occurred about two months after living in Canada, I was driving on the road one day and was seeing two set of white dividing lines. It was actually one line but I was literally seeing two dividing lines. It was a most frightening moment that brought tears to my eyes.

I pulled over off the road and said to myself, " why did I come here"; rehearsing the question that Sheldon my older son asked me. I had no one at the time to relate the experience to because my wife was in the hospital. What do you do in piercing moment like this? As mentioned before all my social support was in Jamaica. Therefore, I had only one who is permanently present who is the closest to me at the moment and all times, who promised that He will never leave me nor forsake me.

I reached to that inner part of me and tears crawling down my face, I cried to God and said, please God help me. That was not one of those religious prayer, it was a desperate call for help. I sat in the car for about 10-15 minutes and drove home while drying and drinking tear falling down my cheeks, wondering what is this mystery.

In my moment of thinking out loudly while driving home, I recalled a song we use to sing in the Franklin Town New Testament Church of God in Kingston Jamaica it came streaming from my heart through silence.

As young man Vidette and myself were members of the youth choir. There were many songs we were taught by brother Leonard Taylor the choir master. The one that gushed out of me in silent melody, in this uncertain moment was: "Through it all, I've learned to trust in Jesus, I've learned to trust in God; I've learned to depend upon his words". This was followed by another outstanding one it was titled "Tears are a language God understand". It says " Often you wonder why, tears come into your eyes and burdens seem to be much more than you can stand but God is standing near; He sees your falling tears; tears are a language' God understand; God sees the tears of a broken hearted soul, He sees your tears and hears them when they fall; God weeps along with man and takes him by the hand; Tears are a language God understand:

When grief has left you low, it causes tears to flow and when things have not turned out the way that you had plan, but God won't forget you, His promises are true tears are a language God understand; God sees the tears of a broken-hearted soul:

He sees your tears and hears them when they fall; God weeps along with man and takes him by the hands; tears are a language God understand".

God reminded me! it could me nobody else to awaken that divine streaming, it came from my innermost being like a flow of cool water to water my soul. He said to me, "I am with you"," I am in you".

My human self was still asking, how do I escape this threat of this physical confusion that has crept into my life. I entered into my inner self and reached that door of hope. It swings open to mental courage and divine consciousness. Him that knew me before I was formed in my mother's womb in quietness sheltered me in that comforting arms.

I surrendered to the only help that was present inside of me still shedding tears the language that he understood. And enter into my inner court, that divine most holy place where God dwells. He who breathes His breath in us and we all became living souls. The "I Am that I Am" who told Moses that I am sending you to the Pharaoh of Egypt as a god to do a deliverance.

I started to evaluate my new reality as a part of my divine destiny. I accentuated that divine being who I am and submit to my change. I sold out to meekness, kindness and constant acknowledgement of my divinity over my humanity. The legend Marcus Garvey said, "man don' know themselves until their back is against a wall". God lives in you and you are the active temple of God and He does not take vacations.

Recognizing your God connection as the extension of who you are is not a religious exercise. It is not about accepting a religion with a man-made rules and labels. It is simple to Love God with all you heart all your soul all your strength and your neighbor as yourself.

By changing your thinking, you can change your complicated circumstances. Your thoughts are the only help you have to reach to your source to transform any situation. It kept me from despair and allowed me to embrace my divinity over my humanity. We are all a part of God and his divine plan.

The Apostle Peter put it this way "Gird the loin of your min'". Get sober! You are not only flesh you are also spirit with a soul within your body. Change can be like a prison but you have the key for all the doors. Just open that door on your inside the answers are in that inner place; that inner court where the soul of man is while living in this tent called body.

When I was in University one of my literature book was titled "man Search for Meaning" by Victor Frankl. He was a doctor, a neurologist and psychiatrist who was captured during World War II. His experience in the concentration camp separated him from his wife and children. He used the term "logotherapy" in his book to highlight that he drew comfort from his thoughts. He drew meaning from his inner self and survived by extrapolating experiences from his life before concentration camp. Th theory is that "Man is deeply motivated to live purposefully and meaningfully; and that man find meaning to life as a result of responding authentically and humanely to life challenges"

I believe that you can survived and overcome your challenges in life by reaching to that source/God connection to the divine self. In my experiences going through my imposed changes, by your human self you are helpless.

Victor Frankl rehearsed the experiences with his wife before they were separated by war. He didn't know if his wife was dead or alive. He said in his book; he clings to the image of his wife although across his mind; he didn't know if she were still alive. He knew only one thing love goes very far beyond the physical person of the beloved. It finds its deepest meaning in his spiritual being, his inner self. Whether or not he/she is actually present. Whether or not she /he is still alive at all, ceases somehow to be of importance. Our thoughts are like bridges to cross over any obstacle.

He put fort argument that it was no difference if she was alive or not, the mental image and the conversation he had with her and the image would be just as vivid and satisfying, '

Songs of Solomon in chapter eight; the Shulamite woman to her beloved states "set me as a seal upon your heart; As a seal upon your arm; For love is strong as death". I mentioned before that I have real conversation with my late wife. The conversations are so intense, real and constructive like she was very present. It convinced me that when you put away this human tent your eternal divine being never ceases to be active because you are eternal.

I drew upon my divine source to overcome my dark experiences. In the times of trouble and psychological imprisonment you can reach to your higher self and find joy in these moments of unpredictability. You can become unstoppable amidst the stress and strains and trials. Just recognizing and acknowledging your divinity as a soul in a body. You can go through without succumbing to the pressure, instead surviving the intensification of change. The great artist and creator are working with as the selected raw material.

In times of crisis the cry can be so loud it drown out the answer to the urgent call for help. Your answers are inside you. Just understand that we live in a universe that love is the ultimate crafts man. That love will take you through the dark paths of life.

When human effort fails just stop; take a breath, open the door on the inside, keep your focus within. That limitless divine presence will emerge from the experience with immense enlightened directions. The answer to your questions that you are agonizing over is on your inside free from the noise of the human. Free from the foggy thoughts that dim the sight of your divine consciousness.

Passionately pursue it from within to draw out that inspiration and it will unfold. You are more divine than human, acknowledging that truth can demystify your story. It is not written in a textbook; it is ascribed on your divine soul made in the image of God. Don't look for what you have lost outside of yourself, open that door on your inside and you will find it brilliantly shinning as the sun.

That is the crucial transformational inside step we need to take on this journey of life for healing of our human scars. You are a divine being! Don't look in the wrong human direction. God will speak to you in silence, listen for that voice from your inner being. You will be vindicated by that divine soul that God breathe in. It is weightless, limitless and eternal and unnoticed by human eyes.

Your reality of abnormality will become normal with your inner change, it's all a part of the plan to purpose. With a new perspective of who you are it will shine a radiant light in your consciousness and evict ego. Your vision will not be blurred any more, the light from your inner court will begin to shine. Jesus said "I am Light of the world" and we are all light of the world 'our beam will illuminate the darkness.

The path became lighted and a new day dawned and your divine miracle will give birth. When you find yourself along the path of desolation on your journey, your corners and dark alleys will change to freeways.

You can turn your human sufferings into divine achievement and divine accomplishment. This is not optimism it cannot be achieved from human potential it is a divine resolve that has its origin from God your divine source.

Your anticipations and aspirations can be manifested, by been implicitly convinced in your inner self that you are not alone in the melting po of life. You are not here by accident but by a divine design that required spiritual energy.

When my family and I migrated, a phyco-social shift took place in our lives. The reality of change hit us at the core of our being. It required mastering our change. We all have to now let ourselves believe what we discover and get the fiction of expectation out of our physic.

Now is time to recalculate our inner thoughts. The situation landed us into a prison of anxiety, that could only be disengaged with an energy deeper than our humanity. The question of who am I? where am I? and why am I here is paving your thought

My inner energy kept me from despair and drove me to search for resolutions. With no immediate social support, it was intimidating. The language of tears, that God understand became my tarmac for courage.

I realized that there was no external solution. Every day I thought about my family who was faced with this new experience without no solid social support outside of the four of us. To compound the problem their mother, my wife was sick the likes of nothing they have ever seen before.

My whole being was saturated searching for answers in a land that I did not know. With all this my thoughts were still actively engaged in search answers. When your back is against the wall your human script is helpless. There is a divine frequency that you have to detect and deliver yourself. Your divine source is the only help in the time of trouble and you know it more when there is no human support.

In these moments when the mind is so actively searching your whole network and mental well-being is threatened. With one wounded soldier you have to be courageous and maintain focus. It dawned on me that true happiness cannot be pursued it must be a decision of your will.

To become depress and carry a sad disposition it is only notice by you. Joy and happiness are like engine oil to keep you going. You cannot make joy; it must evolve from your inner self and be that joy that cannot be erased by any circumstance. Jesus states in the gospel; " your heart shall rejoice, and your joy no man taketh away from you". I was kept by the divine strength that I could only draw from my higher self.

My innate optimism which for many years have been my practice was totally insufficient in the face of tragedy. A Problem cannot be solved by mere optimism it needs divine connectivity. It was acting and acknowledgement of my divinity that propelled me to this new place of consciousness.

When you are confronted with a life that presents shocking unexpectedness and the way you envision is twisted at the curve it is difficult to see the meaning. Your existential dynamics bears severely on your reality. This is a time that calls you to deep evaluation to accept the divine intelligence and affirm that your life is on a path that turns the curve the way it does.

This frustration of adjustment to new realities is extraordinary. During these moths in a new environment with new occurrences in the family; despite the pain and sometime regrets, you find in your higher self that you are capable to withstand the odds.

The lesson to learn from is that life presents shocks that calls for a reinvent and reevaluate your make up. These shocking imposed realities pushed you to set new priorities. This doesn't make you who you are, it reveals how you see you. The vividness of these occurrences' truly forces you to look within yourself and there discover your capabilities.

The universal human paradigm, the whole notion that you by your self can conquer your fate to ensure life turns out the way you want it is a mislaying that inner divine power that is inseparable from the human.

We are all divine being created by God in his own image and enter this universe in humanity. This human construct has a limited time to live. It starts to change as we gradually count the years and it shift its structure with wrinkles and mobility and sometimes cognitions. The limitless, eternal and infinite you that I refer to as "the divine you" possesses a connection to your source. It doesn't ask the question; "what if I fail? What if I made the wrong decision? That is the indomitable you that constantly engage in only the important aspect of life instead of the urgent. This divine you need no invention it has extraordinary omnipotent power. In tears and quiet peace, you will find that you. I found it in my Painful contemplative moments. Peace is the ammunition that slay you in the battle of ego. Peace that presents the transformation necessary to step out in your higher self and accept dying to your humanity.

THE POSSIBILITY AND REALITY OF PEACE

Peace is a winning strategy that will enable you to achieve success through your crucifix experience. When God came in human flesh and He was leaving His humanity, back to His complete divinity, He said "; My peace I leave with you, my peace I give unto you that that which the universe giveth I give to you"

Peace is the greatest gift and legacy that God leave with humanity to be manifested through our divinity. It gives you a new perspective of looking on the world, not through the eyes of its deformity, disasters, distress and disintegration of true relationships. When you walk outside in nature you see the peace of divine connectivity with the winds, the birds the green vegetation, the desert, the ocean and the swaying of life in the branches.

Peace is not flavored with anxieties, instead it empties your mind of the feeling of fear and trepidation. It enables you to take your fill of it and move you into the presence of the source. Peace is your singular therapeutic alternative in time of anxiety. It awakens you to operate in divine silence having inner thoughts that connects with God source.

When you operate as a divine peacekeeper, it engages you to let go and let God. The God who made you and breathe life in your soul to make you a divine being living in human body is forever working in and through peace.

This tranquility performs and directs you in silence to someone outside of your human limitations. Peace does not make alarms it demonstrates in the quietness of your soul and accomplishes unparallel results; "be still and know". The peace that comes from divine source composed you with exquisite calm and equipped you to maintain calm in the mighty ocean of life.

Jesus demonstrated His work in peace with uninterruptable connection to his divine source as He was living in human body. He looked like any other human being but He was serving in His higher self as God in a human tent.

When Saint John heard of His work, he was stunned by what he heard. It generated his curiosity; he sends to find out if He was the one to come or they should look for another. His presence was peaceful without funfair and proclamations. The creator of the whole universe is among us.

Jesus responded saying, "tell John that the blind is seeing, the lame walked, the lepers are cleansed, the deaf is hearing and the dead are raised". He did not blow any trumpet or promote His humanity; He submitted the evidence. You are designed to submit evidence of complete loving service through peaceful production. There is no necessity to be first man or first lady. You are part of the divine paradigm of peaceful operation.

The New Testament said we should operate with the same mind, same heart to achieve the same goal. To be the change, that we need, we must empty ourselves of our humanity and be our true self in divinity. Being human is a temporary devotion to pursue things, like recognition and status and class until you die. You are made in the image and likeness of God to pursue divine accomplishment as an expression of your divinity.

Paul said it this way "I die daily," to self and human centeredness; he added "for me to live is Christ and to die is gain". When the ego that dominate the human being die it expand your divine consciousness to love God; to love yourself and to love your neighbor unconditionally.

If we study the lives of people who does not give place to ego and die to their humanity, they answer the question of what is the ultimate value of life. They gave themselves to complete service to the well-being of the human race without focusing on labels. People like Mother Teresa, The Dalai Lama and certainly many other philanthropists who gave themselves to selfless service.

The human soul will shine its light when we are torn of self and are intensely convinced of who we are as divine being living in our human body. We take ourselves for granted not recognizing our divinity. When we allow inner tension rather than inner peace and the freedom that it generates overtakes us, we give up our divine legacy.

Your country is powerful, your communities are powerful because in them dwells the people of God. God created everything perfect and for good. He will inspire you to move from your existential crisis to peace and freedom. There is no political or religious solution only divine solution living from your higher-self. We all can have peaceful and divine outcome through loving service to mankind.

Every breathe we take is a God given renewal of life in motion. You cannot the outcome of that life that you, it's a God-given access to divine levity. The event of your life is not predetermined by you. Actions taken by you in life are profoundly based on divine vibration. The question is now Why do people do evil things? That answer is based on where you placed the emphasis of you living. Remember we are human and divine being so the synchronicity of being is paramount, to the outcome.

Based on scientific research it is said we have sixteen 16) breathe per minutes, 23,000 breathe per day. Science is not the originator of that breathing fact of life. God carefully thought out this intelligent design of the human being and dwell there if fullness. With all the careful scientific analysis and findings man will never demystify the puzzle of life and win. It doesn't how successful a scientist you are and how many researches you successfully accomplished; you will never come up with all the answers where you can say explain the synchronicity of being.

Remember God says "Be still and know that I AM God". In pure peaceful stillness you set the mind in a control mode that will not allow it to roam to and from. You enable yourself a channel of inspiration and manifestations. Peace is a divine grace that allows you to joyous moments even in times of turmoil.

The creatures in the oceans, in the desert, in the jungle, in this vast universe is for our good. They all exist in peaceful composures we are all extremely unique and special creature of God that cannot be scientifically explained.

God gave us all, things pertaining to life and godliness. He gave us peace as one of the most valuable legacy as I stated before the intensity and the degree of passionate feeling with which we build and hope for your life will not be the only factor in bringing life to ultimate fulfillment.

By allowing your life to be in touch with peace and not ignoring the presence of the divine component, that simple quiet presence it will lose its wholeness. That peaceful posture of recognizing the power of divinity will allow you to find peace and divine freedom.

Your simple have extraordinary appreciation for this vast universe that exist in peaceful wind, water and land is miraculous stillness of creation. Life pays no determined attention to what number of things you require for your living to be meaningful. Meaning is when you surrender to the divine presence in you that will live forever no matter what.

There is a great reward in promoting inner peace through meekness. Peaceful presence evokes a divine connection within those who feel they are lacking and missing the real essence of life. There is no such thing as world peace, when you allow yourself to come fully 'KNOWING" of the design of being in divinity in the tent of humanity.

When you keep on giving away peace it keeps coming back at you that is only closest thing to world peace. Peace is far more than imagination it is a vehicle to wholesome relationships that you will experience on your inside.

This is an amazing universe that lacks nothing and we are all important players under the vast blue sky. Every war, every wild fire, every earthquake, hurricane and tsunami and pandemic are part of God's plan. The universe is held together by the divine Source that same Source we are extensions of and workers with. He made creature in the sea and on the earth to keep it physically clean. You are the spiritually cleaner, preserver and illuminator; you are all the salt and light and peaceful transmitter of the world. Human actions bring pollutions and distortion but God still reigns in the universe whether you believe in him or not He still reign and send rain on the just and unjust. Whether you believe or not he is still that divine presence in you innermost being.

We all have an assignment to offer human service through divine source. It is increasingly clear that we are in one global community and we all are interdependent. The existential realities of humanity are unique and diverse. Therefore, essential role to societies cannot be achieved through instinctual data collection but through consciousness. In order to be true stewards and ambassador of this earth and peoples we must draw from our higher self that transcends human boundary.

God provides all the resources you need to work with, to fulfill meaningful and wholesome existence among your neighbors. It starts fundamentally with Loving God, love yourself, love your neighbor as yourself and love the universe in its perfection. This is the antidote for caring for all humanity and on it hangs all the dynamics of life. It's far more than joining an organization attend the meeting and plan programs that is centered around your group. It is a thoughtless claim that the lack of resources is the cause of human sufferings. The misappropriation and the myopic approach to managing the God's given assets He/she bequeath to mankind to be divine stewards.

He, "provides all things pertain to life and Godliness". Life and Godliness! Not to be unaware of, the proof is existing in your higher self but to be managed with divine insight and not ego.

I don't see where "All" is meant that some must have and others must go without because of geographical locations or socio-economic status. As I have stated there is no political solution to our problems. There is an insidious neglect of who we are, we all have the same divine energy flowing through our being. You are human and you are divine! Every problem requires a divine solution, there is where the resolve is that there is an outcome. When you consider the enormity of the divine resource in you your doubt will eventually diminished.

You are already divinely connected; you are an extension of the infinite creator. The undeniable truth is, that your soul is always and will be always intimately connected to divine Source. It is a human misconception to believe otherwise. You must simply remove from mere belief to "know" that truth. Solomon stated in the old covenant: "the whole duty of humanity is to fear God and keep his commandments". The number one commandment is; To love God with all your heart, soul, mind and strength; and to love your neighbor as yourself", as I have stated several times in the manuscript. Failing in this commandment means total failure in all the others. When you serve God, you serve all humanity because God live in all human beings. None of us are accident we are all God's unique gift to the universe.

God sets up government in all jurisdictions to serve for the good of all people of every ethnicity. It is not to compartmentalize people and ward off tension although that is of valuable importance. We have in many countries, what is called " separation of state and church" this is another mis-conception of stewardship as well as what is the church and what is the state. It is the divine source uphold the universe and sets up authorities.

ACKNOWLEDGE YOUR TRUE SELF!

Our soul is the true essence of who we are and who we are cannot be inseparable of that divine, invisible, weightless existence. This is not about utopia it is the fact that all truth comes from within our higher self. All thinking and thought comes from within;

The bible states in the book of proverbs, "Righteousness exalts a nation, but sin brings reproach". Righteousness has no other meaning but " to be right with God" and I may add whoever you conceived Him to be. remember you are created in His image so we all have him/she in us.

The fullness of life and inspiration come from within the God in you. Jesus said "I Am the way"; I am is the name of God. God said to Moses "tell the people I Am that I Am sent you". In the book of Exodus, in the Old Testament of the bible Moses had a verification and validation dialogue with God.

God told Moses to go to the Pharaoh in Egypt to deliver the Israelites. Moses fled from Egypt after he killed the Egyptian young man and buried him in the sand. This Egyptian youth was being mean to Moses

Hebrew brethren. Now Moses had a miraculous encounter with God who spoke to him from the burning bush. God declared to Moses his identity as the God of Abraham, Isaac and Jacob. God mandated Moses to go to Egypt to confront Pharaoh. Moses raised his human fears and limitations why he was not qualified to execute this task of delivering the people from Pharaoh's oppression.

Moses had an identity predicament; in his illusion he asks God who am I to go to Pharaoh? God affirms, "like a legal oat", saying Moses "I will be with you", "I am in you" I Am always there Moses. It was so with Moses and so it is with all humanity.

As I stared earlier in this writing that God is always with all of us and there is never a time that He is not. God is saying in a present continuous mode I am in you and you will never go alone.

Moses asked God when Pharaoh asked me what is your name what shall I tell him? God Responded that "I MA THAT I AM" sent you and that is my name forever. In Exodus chapter 4; Moses said," God they will not believe me"; God's affirmation was reinforcing divine unshaken truth saying Moses- you are going in divine power.

God asked Moses," what is that you have in your hand". Moses replied, "a rod"; God said" throw it on the ground", it turns into snake. God said "take it up" and it turn into the rod. God now validating his divine power in Moses He said, "put your hand in your bosom" when Moses took it out it was fill with sores. God said to Moses "Put in back in your bosom" and when he took it out the sores were gone.

Moses was still making excuses, he said to God "I am not eloquent" God ask Moses "who made your mouth". Failing to acknowledge the divine being we are and reducing yourself to a mere human is not of God. You are an extension of God who will never leave you nor forsake you who lives in you and makes all things possible.

Jesus as the God-man, came in human flesh He states; "I Am the way, I am the Truth, and I Am the Life".

We are all living as a temporary human but we are forever living as a divine being as an extension of God. You should make no excuses of that truth and deny your divinity. Jesus said in the gospel you must deny yourself. You must live true to your divinity. They crucified Jesus because He acknowledged that He is God.

Some will malign you for acknowledging that you are a divine being but does not change that fact you are more than human being. Men's disapproval of themselves and disapproval of must not disengage you from affirming who you are. This profound embracing of your divinity is not a mote point to debate.

When you enter into that inner and higher self and open the inner door to your inside you find this soul reconciliation. That at-one-ment with God. There is where you can act with unconditional love for all humanity. Your true self will be revealed from your humanity and you will know that your human body is the house the real you live in.

You are the way the truth and the life when you enter into your divinity. You can love unconditionally when you are open to your divine self and it is impossible outside your divinity. "With God all things are possible"

All of us are infinite being thought of and formed before we became flesh and dwell among each other. There are no better than we are all one bearing a temporary housing. You existed before you were formed into your mother's womb. You are living in a perfect environment although your bodies exist in a world with many troubles and decay.

Don't be driven by what you see but by what is observing what you see in the mirror. What you see will just allow you to make comparisons and compete with each other and be dissatisfied with yourself. There are even systemic plots and plans that runs against our equality. You are more than what you see looking back at you in the mirror. Know yourself that you are full of a mass of potential with divine possibilities. Free yourself the misrepresentation that contradicts the truth of you complete being.

Every acclaimed individual athlete, engineer, artists allow their instinct to drive them to escape into their soul being to achieve their goals. This is where we are inspired and driven to great achievements.

You create your success before your start training, studying or practicing. You can decide your better or your worse by bringing yourself to acceptance of your divinity. You hang your trophy of achievement on the walls of your thoughts.

Your thinking mold you into what or who you become in the universe. Having wholesome thoughts is the medal of your existence and self-actualization. You must accept this driving power in you that to experience the transformation, because must be free of ego.

Your Thoughts inspire and transfers that energy field to bring about transformation. It enables you to operate outside of yourself and mount you up with wings like eagle and soar beyond your human confinements and limitations.

You must receive the universe in your hearts as a priceless gift from God. Like a child who receive his or her gift on their special day, they don't think about where it come from or how much labor was put in to buy it.

Jesus said "unless you be as little children, you cannot enter his kingdom". For you to gain your rightful inheritance you must identify with source. You may have made mistakes and bad judgements in your past, make that synchronizing inner move to accept yourself for who you are. The threats of selfish ego to hold you back with lose its power over you.

EMBRACE THE PRESENT

J ust know the past is the past. The past cannot be undone, you cannot reverse what is done already, the present is what you have to work with. Being a divine being is your greatest possession being the extension of God.

The shocking unexpectedness of the passing of my partner and friend moved me intensely to re-invent the reality of my knowledge of life's existence. There was no way to predict or control our destiny together. I could be the one to leave her from this human body. The possibility of all of .us to be confronted with the unexpected is can happen randomly.

What the event and the moments do to me was to placed me in a reflective evaluation. It inspired me to embrace my present as the only tool I have to work with. It inspires me to evaluate my priories and established a new perspective. All or most of your cultural, religious and social fixation was challenged by my present experience.

All of the disquietude that occupied my attention was melting from my inner self. I began to write my present awaken and enlightenment. I stop and consider the potential disagreement or dispute, misunderstanding that this manuscript could proclaim that is counter to traditional accepted belief. I immediately dismissed all outside pressure concluding that they would be trivial to the message of the content of the book.

Whatever you are inspired to do that which is coming from deep inside your soul; whether it will break the rules or investigate the norm be prepared not to die with your divine awaken. It is easier to be remembered for being known for who you really are than avoiding the danger of being rejected for your truth of being and your purpose proclaim.

The human paradigm will always want to pursue what is popular acceptance. You are created to always being in pursuit of divine accomplishment or making your thoughts known of your inspiration. That inspiration is a present moment experience or epiphany. Upon attaining that divine encounter, you will move on in pursuant of gaining the dept divinely achievable graces like loving your neighbor as yourself and loving your enemies. Be cognizant of this, you will never achieve this from a mere human resolve.

YOU ARE AN EXTENSION OF GOD

You are created in God's own image, you are like God, with this mass of intelligence and spiritual insight. What you are trained in at schools, colleges and universities, do not make you who you are. God gave us his intelligent DNA and become active in us to live and breathe.

Jesus in human flesh demonstrated God willingness to dwell with Him as one. He said 'My father and I are one'. The tree and the branches are one source, one root and one origin. He said in the New Testament "I am the vine and you all are the branches". The tree cannot be different from the branches.

God is a spirit with divine attributes, He knows that the human being is finite with limitations. He dwells in you as that spirit with divine attributes so we can be infinite, limitless. You cannot be different from your maker who created you in his own image. You came from the same intelligence.

The apostle Paul, in the New Testament, said "Let this mind be in you that was also in Christ, who being in the form of God, thought it not robbery to be equal with God" .It is perfectly accurate to see God as you instead of an artist imagination or perception. The artist picture of Jesus is loaded with his culture, color and I may add great controversary.

You have the mind of God with active thoughts to be pro-creator with Him as an infinite living being. Do not evaluate yourself based on what you lack, that is transitory, see yourself in terms of your divinity. You have divine characteristics in your soul and it is eternal and formless.

Listen to your inner voice that is repeating this truth quietly that you are a divine being. In quietness and silence, just repeat" be still and know that I am God, you are actually connecting your spirit with God.

In the New Testament it said "Jesus became flesh and dwell among us". In His flesh we see His glory and His divinity that is full of grace and truth. Our putting on flesh, is miraculous as Jesus was conceived miraculously. No human biologist can fully explain how a human being live in water in their mother's womb for nine months. Humanism with its concentration on human activities and possibilities cannot demystify it outside of some dogma. Every individual human being is unique and is an awesome wonder.

Your divine attributes are the only conclusive answer to the cycle of life it is transformational and at the same time its eternal existence. This is the story of existence that no human mind can demystify. God is present in every one of this unique entity call human being all of us are created with divinity. Your divinity allows you to love God with all your heart, mind, soul and strength and your neighbor as yourself. Not loving your neighbor as yourself is expressing that you have not recognized who you really are in divinity. You cannot love God and not loving your neighbor. You have that highest awareness in you just unlock the door on your inside.

Loving God, yourself and your neighbor as yourself is a spiritual ultimate. It cannot be attained through religion. It is the fulfillment of your divine journey of knowing God and not knowing about God. You cannot be separated from this truth; it must be a common thread flowing through your being. Remind yourself that you are created in the image of God who is pure love and you have in you that same pure love.

One of the names of God is Love. God is love and those who love others have God. In 1 John 2, it states that 'I am not writing a new command, but the same from the beginning that we love one another'. This love that you should walk in commanded to, Love God with all your heart, mind, soul and strength, and love neighbor with that same intensity.

No one can stop you from living the love that God commanded us to love in this threefold way. Love is a divine individual initiative that is achievable, not in humanity. Make no excuse to any one that you are a divine being, capable of loving your enemies. It is not by human it is God command that exceeds the physical. You are a divine being and your divine nature will make this possible.

Not knowing who you are can make life difficult because you will not be living to your true potential. You are more a divine being than a human being. Know this truth without a trace of doubt. To be double minded you will be unstable in all that you do.

The threefold command is not about being loving, but to Love like God loves. His love is demonstrated clearly when Jesus came. Love surpass the physical it comes from the divine source. That love will effortlessly flow into the universe through your divine outlet. You are a divine being with the love of God in you. This is not about being baptize and hang on to religion and attend church. Amidst your human weaknesses and errors dwells the love that is God. Open that door on your inside to enable it to become characteristic of who you are

God observed you and the whole universe in its uncontrollable order and made love the theme of order. You are created by God to love; your God consciousness' is to love. Discrimination, racism, classism is divisive and fill with human hate. Deep inside of all of us we are searching for love. Whether we want to admit it or not, we are "loveaholic""; on a perpetual crave to find love and freedom in love and to love.

Crime, violence or war cause you to not operate in your divine love. If you allow these things to hinder your work of love in God, you will lose track of who you are as divine being. Our love for humanity should not be disturbed or restricted based on status, race, skin color, religion, sexual orientation, socio-cultural or socio-economic differences. Deep down inside of us is the imbedded desire to love and be loved. This desire is divinely wired and encoded in our divinity. This programmed love is constantly downloading into our divine being as we live our lives as a human being. It exists there in silence from we were formed directing us to that truth of who we are.

John said in the New Testament 'I have no greater joy than to hear that you walk in truth'. Receive the truth, that you are more a divine being than a human being and walk in that truth.

Tell God about the temptation of your humanity and give up the past, you are unable to fix it. Tell yourself that you are on a new path, and you are a new person and old things have passed and gone. You are divine soul and a part of God. Use your mind to send love to people, even those who don't agree with you. Love does not see the evil or bad habits as deference but aim at the tremendous possibilities that exist in your soul.

Love is the highest and only way to reach the soul of another human being. Through a innermost conversation with yourself you can find that divine love streaming from your being. It is virtually impossible to fully grasped the essence of another human being unless you love that person. Through love you are armed with insight of essential traits and potential in that person.

Saint John 4:7 of the New Testament states "He that loveth not, knows not God for God is love". You must know God to know who you are and how to love. To truly liberate yourself, you must know who you are and know that love is the ultimate way to real freedom.

Jesus was prepared and able when he took on humanity to bring salvation to humanity, because man's salvation can only be realized through love and in love. He knew that he was, truly man and truly God, so He demonstrate divine love in love for humanity. He confirmed this when he said 'I am in the father and the father is in me'. We must come into the full divine knowledge of this sacred truth.

Your humanity is a temporary and decaying part of your being. You are also a divine eternal being that existed before you were thought by your human parents. You have a divine DNA before you enter your mother's womb. Religion is coated and crafted with the potential or ability to rob us of ourselves and place labels on us, you are far more that religion.

Religion and religiosity can be shallow and self- proclaimed and identity crafted it has the potential to divert your divine focus. To be God focus you owe it to yourself to learn by teaching yourselves who you are in the 'I Am 'consciousness.

Jesus said "Be ye doers of the word and not hearers only". What is meant by that is, you should teach yourself by the action. He is declaring to all that you are responsible and must actualize the word through observing the precepts and testimony of the divine. Don't get on an intellectual platform to reveal who you are it is better to discovered from entering into your higher self. It is a soul exercise that allows you to transcend your human existence to your divinity.

One of the fights that exists in religion is to a large extent is perpetuation of another human idea that is counter to the divine truth of God. The religious persons in Jesus time when He was on earth accused Him of breaking the man-made laws.

The divine word always directs us to something or to someone outside of our human self. Don't place emphasis on your humanity but have a true encounter with your source. The more you die to your humanity, you give prominence to your divinity and make love and service your lifestyle.

Humanity says we should love our neighbors but if they are different from you, store them in the cloud until they are like us. Not sharing the same religion and values, they are outcast. Without embracing your way overtime or in time you press the delete button. God's truth is that you must love forgive those who are different and who trespasses against you, no matter what. The human idea is that you take some time to get over your own hurt before you forgive those who hurt you.

You are endowed with limitless energy to raise kindness and unconditional love under all circumstances. Even if the wrong meted out to you is so severe always remember that no one have the right to do wrong. You will not find this energy of kindness and unconditional love in your humanity, it requires divine frequency to move away from revenge to help the weak, love them and live your truth. There is no place for bitterness in your life. In your divine self is the indomitable energy of love and power to forgive. Forgiveness is not an ego effort; it is a divine accomplishment.

Life's experiences are your teacher and all are working for God and for your good. Make a divine evaluation," (not a religious evaluation" and let breaches be a teachable moment and eliminate judgement from your life. Your divine consciousness of thoughts will bear fruit and enable you to make a righteous conclusion. Never justify your bad behavior because injustice was meted out to you. Know that you have the divine energy flowing through you and resentment is not a part of who you are.

You have unlimited energy power to transform your world and to transform others life. Transform meaning to operate outside yourself, outside of your human limitations. Paul said in the New Testament 'Be transform by the renewing of your mind'. As I have stated many times in this book, God said "Love with all our heart, soul, mind and strength and your neighbor as yourself". This is the formulae for transforming possibilities because man can only be delivered through charity and in love without pretense.

It is almost unconceivable to image the profound potential and transformational effects of loving God with heart, mind, soul and strength. It is the right thing to do and it has limitless personal benefits for all humanity. This is a matter of the heart and soul emerging for source.

When you are fully absorbed about somethings, some of your expressions are as following: this is coming from my heart; this is a heartfelt thank you; this love is from deep within my heart; I put all my heart into it etc.

The human heart is a very complex organ in the central nervous system. It is a large muscle that pumps around the blood for circulation through all veins and capillaries. The heart has tremendous impact on the complete state of our mind and body system and all its workings. Many times, we are given the impression that the brain is the organ that is responsible for the bodily reactions to stimulus by interpreting the messages and signaling responses via the central nervous system.

New research has revealed that the heart actually has its own logic that often deviate from 'standard' director of communication in the central nervous system that goes from brain to body. It also highlights the view that it not only communicates information physically to the brain through complex neutral path but also through electromagnetic field interaction. The human heart is a power house in the human body, it is the most powerful and most extensive organ in the human body. The heart in many senses is far more than just a mere organ. It also operates as an actual endocrine gland that secretes hormones various supreme functions. The heart controls the human body functions.

On the other hand, the soul transcends the heart, it exists before we put on flesh and born into the universe. The soul is weightless, invisible, limitless, eternal and divine, it operates from the God center. The heart, operates from the human center, it is the super power of the human body. However, it will stop functioning one day; it will have pains and troubles in the course of man's life. On the other hand, the soul is superior to the heart, the heart will stop but the soul it is eternal and is limitless, and existed before you were formed in your mother's womb. The soul is eternal and cannot be explained by any kind of scientific analysis.

The soul is infinite, it has no beginning and has no end. God knew the soul before we were conceived to enter the world as human beings. The indisputable truth is that we are more spirit than flesh. You existed before the foundation of the earth.

According to scientific research the heart has a mass quantity and weigh less than one pound according to scientist. Your soul is, formless, limitless, non-mass and is eternal. There are numerous researches about the heart by many scholars. They say that the heart has its own intuitive knowing i.e. to know something we don't ponder or sit and think about. We are familiar with the term "I knew from my heart" In contrast, the soul is that eternal all-knowing presence that is divine and interact with God.

The body that you came into this world with, is not really who you are, it changes as we go through the life cycle. The body is a temporary house for your divine soul. Paul said in the New Testament 'your body is the temple of the Holy Spirit'. God standard is that you love yourself, appreciate the tent but operate within your divinity. It is through your body that your eternal soul manifest in acceptance of its divine attributes. Whether you are black, brown or white, love yourself because the real you are colorless and all are equal.

Some people came in the world blind, dumb, deft and other physical or mental challenges. That is not who they are the reality of who they are existing as a supreme and transcendent being. You are the extension of God, living in human form. Your self-worth is your responsibility, be acceptance of who you are even with physical challenges. Consider yourself worthy to be formed and born. Know that you are not a victim but part of God's divine plan and that you are a perfect being in divinity. Never depend on others to validate you, it is your self-worth that will verify who you are. It is called self-worth because it is your innate responsibility to know that you are worthy. Never see yourself as provisionally existing, you are whole divine being.

If someone say unworthy things about you, don't accept it. This is only their opinion of you, their opinion doesn't make you who you are. If someone say worthy things about you acknowledge it and say thank you.

Self-worth is to accept with full conviction that you are worthy of being. It is not called others-worth it is your own worth, so you must own it and treasure it.

Likewise, self-esteem is you esteeming yourself as an extension of you source. There are difficult human external circumstances that may be in opposition to the norm, that is socially accepted. See that situation as opportunity to grow spiritually far above your human being. Self-esteem in not others giving their opinion about you nor telling you who you are. Self-esteem is not about empty boasting and self-promotion; it is about having an honest truth of ones-self.

AFFIRM YOURSELF AS DIVINE

Never see others as better than you. We are all special in God's divine establishment. We are all created with a divine soul, connected to God our source. No need to add or subtract anything from who you are to be like someone else; your true self is within. Open the door on your inside and you will find your true identity it is a thought inside you.

We are all unique individuals, fearfully and wonderfully made in the image of God however you conceived Him/Her. Make no excuse for your race, colour or ethnicity. We are all divine being all living in human flesh that changes through the cycle. Shift the way you think about yourself; it will change your life.

You should at all times affirm yourself as an extension of God. Know who you are and love yourself. You must know profoundly and intelligibly, that you have a divine right to be happy in your humanity. Your divine attributes enable true happiness because happiness is a decision of the will to be. It is not based on some external good. Make being happy a way of life, don't tie your joy and happiness to any past or future, that would be imposing on the present. The reality of the present must not be overlooked it is the building blocks for attaining your human potential and to grow in your divine self.

Jesus said: "happy are the meek for they shall inherit the earth". Seeking others approval is a way that destroy and disturb your happiness. Be happy even if man revile and persecute and speak evil against you. Don't depend on other people's approval to be happy; someone else is not responsible for your happiness. Unhappiness is a departure from your normal function and the inability to cope successfully to the demand of the environment. Happiness is a decision of your will that has its resolve in the higher self.

You are in charge of your self-esteem. You have the right and responsibility to esteem yourself; to accept you for who you are. It is good to esteem others; it does make you feel good about yourself as well as making others feel good about themselves. But don't only feel good, know that your good. Don't live waiting for others to give you approval. You are ultimately responsible to build your own self-esteem and love yourself.

The New Testament said you should esteem others better than yourself because people know things and know how to do somethings better than you. In other word we are all unique entity with different abilities so we should give recognition to other people's uniqueness. However, that does not make you less than them because you also have your special ability and to love others as you love yourself. It does not mean you must neglect your obligation to esteem yourself. Be appreciative of others because we are all interdependent being.

You will also find things that you can do better than other people. That don't make you better than them. You are not what you can do, not what you own nor what you achieve. You are a divine being in a human tent with tremendous divine capabilities. Rid yourself of any self-defeating attitude that will come to your thoughts. Seek to be inspired, which means, I repeat; to be in-spirit and walk in spirit instead of manifesting your ego.

Never carry around guilt in your life, it can diminish your self-esteem. If you did something wrong, forgive yourself of the past it happened already. If you hurt someone, ask them for forgiveness and move on, you cannot change what happen its done. Do not remain in guilt, even if they refuse forgive you. You have done what you can do about the situation and it cannot change, though it may cause pain to others. Do not give anyone control over your life because you did them wrong, forgive them and forgive yourself. Be assured in your soul that you forgive them and be totally exonerated, after you have repented in your spirit.

If you keep unforgiveness in your heart, you are destroying your physical body and your spiritual freedom. Forgiveness can only be streamed by divine energy and frequency. You don't have any control over the other person but you have control over yourself to turn to goodness and mercy. Change the way you go forward and refuse to worry. Worry it is a waste of mental, emotional and spiritual energy. It will not change any situation in your life, it is just a bad habit that will poison and eventually destroy your physical body.

Always be aware of the fact that you are a divine being and you can cast all the cares of life on God. It does not matter how much energy you put into worry; it will not reverse what has already been done. Move on with confidence and freedom will emerge in the spirit and by the spirit.

Your infraction is yesterday; it will not turn back and it will not come again even if the same thing happens tomorrow or next week or next month it is all new every time it occurs. Your now is today, enjoy the freedom of having today and be grateful and resolve to live peaceable with all. Tomorrow is not here; you cannot do anything about tomorrow, live in the present. Jesus said 'Take no thought about tomorrow', it will provide for itself. The reggae legend Bob Marley songs "Don't worry about a thing, because every little thing is going to be alright". Never keep yourself trapped in the past; it is gone never to return. Be inspired by the present and do not get anxious about the unknown tomorrow. If you want to be great, you must use the divine power that is within you to forgive.

Seek to love in all circumstances and know you are an extension of the divine God. Affirm yourself as a divine being; not to convince other that you are but to know its truth. Affirm yourself as a spirit in human form, not to get others to follow but to know it to be divine truth. Some may see your truth as a shift because religion has sold God as an abstract figure that will come down from, "heaven" to us. The question is; why if you shift from a "standard" view you can be seen as anti-religious. We live in an expansive and changing world, we are even told that there are "alternate truth". There is a human freedom that cannot be snatched from you, that is the freedom to choose, whether it is truth or alternate truth. That freedom does not change the fact that there is a God who create us all in His own image and God is a spirit; "they that worship Him must worship Him in spirit and in truth".

This truth has no alternate truth and cannot be change by man's whims and fancy. That truth is, we ae are divine soul created by God living in a temporary human body that will decay but a divine weightless, limitless and changeless eternal soul. You are not what you have, where you live or what educational status you achieved. Not the trade or profession you choose, those does not make you who you are. These things will fade while your eternal soul will live throughout all eternity. One must choose their guiding truth by knowing and not mere believing. Believing is only an intellectual comfort zone that is rooted in human theories. Knowing is experiencing truth through inspiration.

Your higher self is infinite and eternal, whatever else is it is temporal, finite and is bound by time. You have that divine energy that flows through you to engage you in a higher consciousness. Inspiration is the source of all invention; this divine energy is the builder of your strength and character. This divine energy allows you to affirm profoundly what the Apostle Paul says in the New Testament 'You are more than a conqueror through him that love you'.

Release your closed culture and beliefs and advance to know your divine self and divine truth. It is your divine thoughts that will reveal who you are to yourself and to the world. Accept divine peace as the provision to put purpose to your life. Peace is a divine legacy that placed you in a higher purpose of living. Paul said in order to reach his full divine potential and purpose "I Die Daily". You must die to self to have unlimited divine energy and creativity. "You are the salt and light of the world" said Jesus you have tremendous transformational potential.

1 Corinthians 15:28 Paul states "When all things shall be subdued unto him, then shall the son also himself be subject unto him that put all things under him that God may be all in all". For God to be all in us, we must live our divinity beyond the human body. In verse 39-40, he added all flesh is not the same flesh :but there is one kind of flesh of men, another flesh of beast, another of fishes and another of birds.; There are also celestial bodies and bodies terrestrial: but the glory of the celestial is one, and the glory of the terrestrial is another" Jesus said it in the gospel "If any man will come after me, you must deny self" i.e. to be

like me and live in divinity clothed in humanity and fulfill the purpose of God, as" Emanuel"-meaning "God with us".

In verse 45; Paul continued, "The first Adam was made a living soul; the last Adam was made a quickening spirit. verse 47-49, ' The first man is of the earth, earthy; the second man is the Lord from heaven. As is the earthy, such are they that are earthy and as is the heavenly such are, they also that are heavenly. And as we have borne the image of the earthy, we shall also bear the image of the heavenly."

VALUE YOUR DIVINITY

K now and trust the fact that you are a divine being. Your divinity means you are connected to God/Love/Source. 'I am in you and you are in me' said Jesus Christ of Nazareth in the gospels.

Love is a divine characteristic of God; it is the very nature of God. Love must define you as a divine being because you are an extension of God. Love is that energy coming from your soul which enables you to demonstrate unselfish inner empathetic concern for the well-being of others. To serve others without conditions, it must vibrate from your innermost being. People who are different from you and have different values and beliefs, you will be able to send them love instead of criticism through that divine vibration. They may believe different from you; they may look different from you, speak different from you; their values might be totally opposite to yours, but they too are an extension of God.

Never cast judgement on others, let love overthrow any contemplation to pass judgement on anyone. Judgement belongs to God because only Love/God knows humanity completely. Fill your soul with love, peace, joy, kindness for others and God will seal your instructions. Love must be your compelling motivation to serve your neighbors. St. John 4:18 states, "There is no fear in love, but perfect love drives out fear."

Clearly authentic love knows no boundary, have no conditions, it is open and real. It overcome fear and it is not looking for conspicuous rewards. As your divinity expand in your consciousness you will find it easy to love as God love. This is a way to deny self, crucify flesh and live from your higher self. To advance your life to the place of your true meaning you must see humanity through love. Love cure all hurt, destroy jealousy, respect all people and feels others pain. The intensification of divine love gives you the empathetic pull to respond to the cry of your neighbor.

The hymn "Amazing Grace" was composed by a young 22 years old – American man by the name John Newton. He was in the business of selling slaves. John Newton would travel to West Africa on his ship and carry these men and women to South Carolina to live sub-human lives. One day while travelling across the ocean, a storm developed. He heard a load scream from one of person he was carrying in his boat to sell as slave. This scream awakens the divinity within John Newton, he pondered it in his higher self while he was waiting for the storm to stop. John heard the cry and felt the pain and it struck the divinity cord in him and shift his thought, to a response of love.

After the storm he turned the ship around and headed back to West Africa. He took out an envelope and wrote the words for the song that we all sing lustily "Amazing Grace, how sweet the sound that saved a wretch like me". During your storm you can peace and love when you open the door on your inside that can change the course of your actions

During the storm, John Newton had time to ponder and the God that lives in him, stirred his soul through nature to make a right about turn. Consequently, he drove his ship back to West Africa and released the living souls in human body to their freedom. He gave up his slave trade business and became an ardent advocate for the abolition of slavery. This serve as a lesson to all – never give up on those who pursue evil. Send them love, through your divine channel because it can bring ultimate salvation, as I stated earlier. Just one injection of a divine consciousness can stop anyone in the middle of any turmoil and change their direction. One strike of Love and compassion can give you a profound inspiration to serve others. Nature has a way to connect you to divine consciousness; the glory of God is made manifest through nature daily.

Living from your higher self is where love in that moment in time will choose to respond with compassion. A supernatural intervention penetrates John Newton's soul trade and inspired him to change business product. His divine being transformed his thoughts while God was demonstrating His power through the storm. One scream from the soul of another human being connects with John Newton inner self. That shout electrified him to change his trade from selling slaves to love his neighbor as himself. With that divine enlightening does awaken love and enable God in manifest from his innermost being. The scream from one soul transformed John Newton from promoting human bandage to be trail blazer for freedom.

After the raging storm, as stated above; John Newton turn around the ship and sail back to Africa and leave all the potential slaves who were still alive into a position of choice. He then sailed to England docked the ship and gave up his slave trade and start to win men and women for Christ. John's talent was misplaced and clouded in his humanity until one incident of a scream from a human soul ignites his soul into divine consciousness. That divine connectedness will effortlessly engage you to your God given responsibility to choose unconditional love.

Operating from deep divine consciousness it evoked a pure stillness in a soul nature: your manifestation of peace and gentleness naturally occur. Your core being is like a source of love with that deep desire to love unconditionally. The opposite is when you exploit others, you are acting selfishly and not thinking of the well-being of the others person. With this enlightenment and awakening to your divine responsibilities it will inspire your value system and the value you placed on others. That will push you to your higher and most fulfilling experience of life, to love God with all you heart, soul, and strength and your neighbor as yourself. The unconditionally loving experience of being divine will enable you to celibate life and awaken that stillness and let God.

You were born to experience life in its unfathomable silence, peace and love flowing through you being. That caring and other oriented nature and nurture with consideration for others even if they don't look like you or agree with you will be that amazing manifestation of Source. The divine being you are will open your eyes to be bridge builder for people of different creed culture and ethnicity. The unity of the human being with the divine being will sensitize you to be that invisible indwelling spirit inspiring you to peaceful comfort. It will be this magical synchronicity of being with this profound awareness of your God given purpose to the human race. When you service is prompted by your divinity you know the connectedness of all humanity to God and nature and nurture.

The psalms said, "The heaven declares God's glory and the firmament shows the work of God's hand". God communicates to us through nature, in His own unique ways to turn tragedy and pandemic into triumph and rewrite your story. Let this truth sink deep in your heart, that all is well and all things is unfolding as it should. This world that we live in is directed by divine intelligence because there is a higher power, an all-knowing Source energy flowing through the universe. You are all living breathing divine soul created by God in His own image.

You can inhale the calm of God's glory when you take a walk, sail or ride into nature. You can live your divine values when God connects you to himself through natures action and activities. Your divine intelligence will come alive in any storm because natural disasters and tragedies intensify your inner consciousness and awareness to a greater in every life on earth. This intensification push humanity to come together and find answers and solutions from emptiness, despondency and spiritual hemorrhage. Compassion will come alive when fervent love is awakened within your soul. When your human limitation falls short of God/Love, divinity will come alive and move to great divine accomplishment. This is the time you acknowledge your human limitation and that you are living in spiritual poverty and rise to divine consciousness. As Paul said "If you live according to the flesh you will die; but if you live by the spirit, you put to death the deeds of the body and live".

Your aggression and misguided effort can be redirected when spiritual self is manifested with full divine access to divine creativity. A psychotic individual may lose their dignity of human being but they are more than their illness, hidden in you is that silent divine treasure of being. In the same way man has the ability to behave like a dragon and to behave like an angel. Man is created with both potentials, the one he put in active engagement will determine what comes out. Many times, human is pushed into anti-social behavior by different reasons, like abuse, lack of guidance and societal pressure that rob him or her of conscious development.

Counselling and opening of a conversation about their experience and dilemma can redirect that person to his or her higher self to make their own spiritual solution. Every problem and human distortions require spiritual solution and not by external man-made mechanism.

Human experiences with its multi -facets of causation enforced different feelings and reactions to social behaviors. The feeling of nothingness and meaninglessness will give people a sense of hopelessness and let them feel like living is not worthwhile. This kind of anti-social thinking comes out in their behavior that robs them of the true essence of who you are. In many cases some don't have the means to live by and it manifest into human aggression because of socioeconomic situation.

I remember in 2003 I was a project officer in the northwestern area of Kingston Jamaica, where I learned of a group of fearless young men who called themselves " nah liv fe, nothin" In their opinion, they felt their life worth nothing to live for; so they did not care if they die or live, consequently they manifest aggressive behavior.

This is oversimplification themselves and an erroneous identification of who they are. Lack of opportunities for their socioeconomic development was one of the human forces behind this thwarted view of themselves. This kind of thinking was characteristic of this community and results in mutual aggression. In the human physic there is a tendency to render one's self useless, this kind limitation is a reality shared by many strata of societies.

On the contrary, the divinity within has limitless power and possibilities to reach to your higher self and greater value to life. There are scores of stories from people from similar socioeconomic situations who reached into their inner self and resolve to emancipate themselves from that human trap. Your awareness of your divine intelligence can inspire you to be light in new frontiers. In many experiences we have seen many from those communities rise from this so-called meaninglessness to profound inspiration to become successful trailblazers. Hopelessness can become a myth when you reach to your divine self and access divine intelligence to change aggression and depression to human service.

Self-assurance and self-confidence walk shoulder to shoulder, they cannot be bought nor legislated. You can find unimaginable strength in your inner self. There is a higher power inside of you because the creator intend life to be a spiritual experience. You can transform innovative thoughts that is found in the deepest part of your innermost being into actions. Embracing the fact that you are created in the image of God as an extension of God you know that you can handle any challenge. your economic situation has not claim on you to cultivate aggression and any mal-adjustment. You were created in the image of God and endowed with divine power and endless possibilities exist in you. You must walk mindfully of these facts that you ae weightless, limitless and more than overwhelming conqueror.

When you take a wide view of the world you know that your perspective is unique and distinct but developmental. Your spirit is what make that distinction because no other sees exactly what you see, that is why you are enabled to make decision for you. The flesh is in constant fight against the spirit but deep in your uniqueness can tell what you think no one else can. Your soul and your spirit are the thinking center of your being that limitless part of you allow you make conclusions.

Your body will change as the years passes but your soul is eternal and changeless. We are infinite being, we are weightless but we focus on the changing finite human part of who you are. Your finite human nature is where build and enable aggression and emptiness. When you live in the higher power and intelligence you can reach to orgasmic feeling of peace flowing spontaneously from deep inside your being. That experience aligns your soul to that ultimate awakening to love as God loves. You see life in its destiny form and everything is predestinated and you are living in your destiny. I saw that kind of thinking and mindset comes out in my late wife Vivette through her sufferings. She would say time and time again quote: "I have a thing with God we talk like friends". She would express that such validation and calm enthusiasm like she was caught up in the rhapsody of her divine self. Paul in the New Testament said "All things work together for my good".

The weightless, invisible part of us is who we are, that limitless observer of the image we see when we look in the mirror. Let us not define ourselves as that tangible obvious being that look back at us in the mirror. You are more of what you cannot see in the mirror of life. There is the silent observer looking back at you and saying, "peace be still". That observer exists before you were formed in your mother's womb and knows everything about you.

We have come to believe that we are who and what other people or society think of us. Fighting and strife overtakes your humanity as you take a ride in the park of ego. The desire for validation from others is not necessarily a bad thing but one must not live with that expectation. Never become dependent on other people's opinion to validate who you are. You must affirm and accentuate your divinity as Jesus did when he was in human body. He came as Emmanuel in human flesh as demonstrated in the New Testament accounts in the scriptures. He was rejected by many but He did not lose focus of who He is as the divine son of God.

They had wide and varied opinions about Him and who he is but he maintained his divinity existing in humanity. What you are or who you are is not what others think of you. You must know yourself as a part of God's divine love clothed in human flesh. Never let your ego push you to seek approval from or of man, you are a divine being. Jesus's constant was love even in rejection, abuse and injustice.

God wants us to love each other's and by virtue of that, we are loving Him. Love even those who you may consider not deserving of your love. Love comes from God and God is love, you are all a part of God's divine creation. The scripture states "God commends his love to us, while we were still violators of the law". He sends Jesus to die for humanity, so you can have unconditional love for your neighbor. All things are possible because we are created a perfect divine being, living in imperfect human body. This perspective allows you to accept your present position where others see complexity and inaccuracy of themselves.

Fill your subconscious with joyful expectations and let love be that driving divine energy that you broadcast from. Be passionate about the present it is all you have to work with and let love be the highest and ultimate motivation. It is tempting to call the past the good old days but the past has served us and prepared us for the present. "All things work for you good," affirm and imbibe that truth. Discard any path that leads you to nowhere, take the freeway to love. This path will take you home to who you are as a divine being. Block any thought process that will bring you confusion and self-condemnation. Deep inside your higher self-lives that divine intelligence. Never travel the path of ego it will lead you to perpetual lack of your true self.

Find love in who you are as that divine being that took on temporary human being. Don't replace who you are, defuse the thought that wants you to become someone else God created you perfect. Find comfort and satisfaction in you. Transcend ego and live in the spirit to unveil that infinite divine being you are. Your mental, emotional and physical fights is to enlighten you to open the door to your inner courts. In that room on your inside is the eternal soul that is full of love and life. There is an indomitable spirit in you that in charge of all your being. Don't replace her with human limitations which manifest in aggression, oppression and addiction.

In this generation the empirical data shows more violent and oppressive behavior and desperation of the human heart. Human seemingly get addictive to their beliefs and turn to hate, terrorism and all kinds of evil motivation. Human is willing to strap bomb on themselves to display their hate and aggression. There is a wholesale devaluation of human lives that come from human ego. Some get addicted the sex and pornography and technology that give less room for conversation and social interaction.

Have deep conversations with God, whoever you conceived Him to be. First see Him as the being that you are created in His own image. You can see that divine intelligent source like you see you. He speaks to us in silence and in love. Don't get preoccupied with asking him for things instead, ask him to inspire you to serve others. Serving others will bring tremendous joy and incalculable satisfactions. Service to humanity will manifest immeasurable transformation, as you are operating outside your human limitations. Your heart will be made glad in loving service to humanity. Know love personally not about love only inter through it and serve with enthusiasm. Celebrate life through loving service, real love will advance life to its crescendo. Enjoy this priceless gift call life, you were created to enjoy this divine experience don't let the human rob you of the miraculous soul you are.

Just see the present, the now as your success story, you all your senses are intact. We live in dichotomies, there is insufficiency in human and at the same time there are unlimited potential in the same person. When he or she rise to the higher self you will find beauty, love and freedom. You don't have to be what others say or think about you. That is called peer pressure and anything that comes through pressure cause pain. You were created to enjoy peace, freedom and in a state of awe; Psalm 139: 14 states "you are fearfully and wonderfully made"; means you are an awesome wonder. Live with this deep inner connection to be overtaken with joy. The proverb, states; "a merry does good as medicine". You can feel so joyful that in that experience tears flow from your soul through your eyes. You can experience and enjoy multi-dimensional joy from your most inner being. Orgasmic joy that no man can take away from you.

Your success is within you where God dwells as that invisible presence. Look at the big picture of your inner self. You have unlimited energy to destroy aggression, oppression and addictions. You are a divine being manifested in flesh, the inner God who dwells in you is permanent and changeless.

Live with delight, with a grateful attitude. Exit the survival mode, you are a divine spirit being created in the image of God make yourself known as light source. God is in you, be awaken to that divine reality. Help others to understand that you live in a perfect universe and you are endowed with strategic thinking to fight any battle without physical ammunitions.

Trust you divine intuitive and insight it is God speaking to you in silence. Listen to that silent voice that speaks deep inside you. Write on your heart the disclosures you gain from listening to that divine intelligence.

Although you may not be able to explain it rationally you exist in pure love. Let go off your ego and let God divine love flow from your inner most being. Love is the best cure for any hurt and distraction of the human challenges. Remember there is a divine intelligence agenda in every situation, there is nothing you cannot accomplish in time and through love.

As the New testament puts it "All things work together for our Good". You are God's masterpiece, when men despise you, just affirm your divine self with deep clarity of mind. Do it with great enthusiasm- "i.e.

with the God in you". You are a divine being and not only a human being and you are here to celebrate who you are.

Do not hang onto past pain, abuses or misfortune, you are an overcomer the past is gone. Live in the now it is a precious gift from God/Love. Let go of your distorted history and start a conversation for healing and transformation

Your race, color, or socioeconomic status does not define you. You are a part of the beloved, created as perfect soul living in human body. You are special and all the others are the same special hand made of God. There is no one better than the others. Have a deep conversation with God. He is telling you in silence, you are my beloved and I am well please.

There is an inherent danger when over and over you go to prayer and express passionately nothingness and that there is no good in you. Think through your prayers have a real conversation with that indwelling presence. Remember God made you and said it was good. There is always good deep inside. As mentioned before; psalm 139 :14 "You are fearfully and wonderfully made"; you are God's hand made. You are unique and strong, that's wholesome thoughts to give the sub-conscious mind to work with. The teachings or beliefs system that man is nothing but biological, psychological, social and genetical, such analysis of humanity lacks completeness. Man transcends the external, outer influences. Human beings are finite and limited but in that human body is the divine soul.

Man's freedom comes from within his divine being. Freedom is one of the highest pursuits of man it is more than arbitrariness and lacks physical barriers. God is this freedom presence intrinsic and inanimate source inside of you. He plays the central role in your life; Paul put is in the

New Testament "In him we live and breathe and have our being". Our story is not fiction, you are divine, that's who you are not mere physical.

There is an antagonistic energy that is opposed to your divine soul. On the contrary there is a peaceful freedom presence of God working in you. Those external forces are opposed to peace and freedom and to conceal the truth of your divinity. That negative oppressive energy work desperately and cunningly to distort your divine inner source and allow you to glory in your humanity.

There is no glory to be experience in your humanity it is a spiritual manifestation. We must be sensitive to the divine perfection within us. It takes a deep awareness of God in you to uncover and accept and find peace in the truth of your divinity.

Through healing ourselves from human ego, the perfection of God will become evident through love. We are schooled by distractions to see ourselves through religions, traditions and cultures. You transcend those human clarifications of who you are, that just allows you to part functional. There is a deeper and silent inner resilient power that worketh in us, an energy assigned to our soul that excels our ego.

Our highest purpose of is to explore life's journey through inspirational awakening. We have traditionally, religiously and culturally unconsciously allowed our minds and thought process to by illusion. To think we are mere human and our true salvation will only come about through some religiosity. God's method is to acknowledge Him and, "be still and Know".

You can overcome the antagonistic plot against the will of the soul by surrendering to God's divine control. He is the main character in your life, active and inspiring to engage you into creative answers. The centerpiece of your story is the will to unlock this divine truth. That truth is that you are truly more divine than human and in you is power to overcome. You can be a host to God who lives in you or you can be a hostage to your traditions and ego. Be the host to God and you will experience that peace that Jesus promised when he gave up his humanness and return to His divine identity.

YOUR INDIVIDUAL INSPIRATION

To be inspired, is to be in-spirit, not some kind of religious outburst to be a spiritual competitor. I am suggesting that we enter into our true higher self and manifest love for God, self and neighbor. To be creative from your innermost being and be impactful to others and that comes through divine inspiration. Every great achievement on the planet is an inspired outflow from the inner being. This opening of the inner door of on your inside starts a divine engagement with God.

People who may display aggression, being oppressive and antagonistic in the universe get inspired at times. They may write a book, sing a song, give a speech or write a movie and so on. Everything that exist on the planet begins with a thought or idea, there is a genius in all of us. The soul stimulates strategic thinking that give birth to ideas and actions. Your thoughts invoke and provoke your will and talents that will ultimately manifest into actions and creativity. It is the energy of the divine spirit that inspires you to build on your thoughts and create in arts, sciences, be a great singer, dancer, writer and all the other creative displays.

Your thoughts give you a quantum leap into your divine ability. As soon as you start thinking the creative energy comes alive. It is important to construct wholesome thoughts. The proverb said "as a man thinks in his heart so is, he". Unwholesome thoughts will also bring results that will not be conducive beneficial to sacred enlightenment. We are thinking beings, therefore the way you think can determine your results. It is the spirit that gives life to every good intention and invention. It does not matter your religious and educational achievement and moral persuasion you are a thinking being. When you are inspired your total being transcend human limitations. Your human body is cast aside and your thoughts ascends to this pivotal awakening that transcend the finite human confines.

This inspiration opens your soul to all kinds of possibilities because the perfection in you explore your inner highest self. Paul said in the New Testament; "whatever things are true; whatever things are honest; whatever things are just; whatever things are pure; whatever things are lovely; whatever things are of good report; if there are any virtue and if any praise, think on these things" Philippians 4:8.

The ability to love unconditionally and the potential to fulfill virtuous qualities will be irreversible in your life. It will make indelible impact on humanity when you develop this soul thinking. These virtues will soften you to a spiritual ascension that supersedes human ego.

One of your primary purpose of existence on this planet is to fulfill your divine love. Such aspiration, however must take into account our human capacity and make that self-detachment to divine acknowledgement. The capacity to detach from one self, is a call to a full surrender of ego. In the book of Romans, the Apostle Paul urged his readers to "present their bodies a living sacrifice". You must come to grip with the fact that every human being on this planet earth is divinely connected. WE have to ugly history where people were and still is treated different because of the color of their skin; their choice of religion; sexual orientation and even geographical location. This thinking has created a psychological warfare for centuries. Such a practice has been normalized by human establishments. It has and continue to generate conflicts throughout the world. To cure this huge dilemma cannot be generated by social and economic strategies, because it is a mindset that permeate the givers and the receivers. To be emancipated from this sensitive human poison it needs a divine transformation to peace and freedom with this divine paradigm shift take place in the human it will bring healing and peace to nations and peoples. To experience this divine perfection, on the inside there must be a dying to the humanity and its norms. I am not talking about some religious revival nor ecumenism. It is submitting the fact that no human shines the sun and light the moon and carry the rain and that every man is created in the image of God and is an extension of that divine source.

Jesus died to his humanity and leave us peace that will enable us to have this consciousness of our divinity. He told us to occupy and to serve and we will do greater works. Your divine spirit can solve any problem and distorted view of yourself and others. There are many available excuses that will present itself to explain why you are a victim of your behavior. But fundamentally it is a lack of embracing and acceptance of your divinity and live by that.

How does one move to accept and embrace his or her divinity? Especially if you are told that you are not good and the closest you can reach to being better is through religion. Therefore, you are imprisoned by this existential crisis. The change from that human existence is to concrete meaning of your identity and the will to find who you are is through divine acknowledge of God in you. Your thoughts and your will to unfold your true self cannot be achieve through mere religion. Religion can be used as the means to or the road map but identifying with extension of God in you is the ultimate victorious life from within.

"Let the weak say I am strong". This is a biblical injunction in Joel 3:10, supported in the New Testament by Peter and Paul; Peter was sent to the Jews and Paul sent to the gentiles. Peter was a fisherman and Paul was a scholar. They both went on a divine mission to deal with an existential problem. What they had in common? They acknowledged their divinity; they were both "filled with the spirit." They went to these two group of people to bridge the segregation.

You can enter into the realm of the spirit and destroy condescending thoughts. Live in perfect harmony with that God connected energy of unconditional love. The quality of your life is dependent on your thoughts. Your battle of the mind is never over but you greatest is to stay divine; Jesus of Nazareth did it and God said He was well please. Your accolades are assured after the performance, God will be pleased with. The war you are fighting is a non-violent one with your inner divine ammunition of love unconditionally.

You can experience peace in turmoil. Place your thoughts in the divine inner courts of you being. As you change your mental attitude you change your circumstances and your solutions will be manifested.

Never assign blame to anyone for what you are going through. Take the lesson, do the test and achieve your just reward of inner freedom. Send love to those who created the problem because hate and anger will deteriorate your human stability. Take no offensive position; choose not to be offended by other's actions or their beliefs and opinions. Carrying resentment is shutting down your divine self. You are a part of God and God is love and that God love is totally unconditional.

Thoughts of anger, resentment for those who wrong you is imposing on the legacy of peace. Peace and unconditional love in the times of great dilemmas and disturbances are like a stream in a dessert. Treat yourself and act as a divine being living in a tent call human. Be inspired always to love and love with great enthusiasm. Let the God in you enable you to bury ego every day and give it no root in your life. Replace ego with God's unconditional love working through to reach those who are hard to love.

Remember you are always connected to God, there is no time that you are not. With God all things are possible. You are guided by divine energy; that is the energy of love and selfless compassion. Freedom is your ultimate destiny and peacefully contenting assured you of the glory.

If you think what you are reading is possible, don't only think, know it is possible. If you think it can bring transformation it will, according to the power that worketh in you. You can rise above being imprisoned by beliefs that put chains on you. Your thoughts can elevate you to live in knowing you are created by a divine source and you are not fighting alone. You cannot be different and separate from your source. God cannot be outside of you; He lives in you. He breathes in you his life and you became a living soul.

Embrace your divinity and live above the trial because the glory will come because no weapon formed can win. Stand up as God-man and stand up against every thought that threatens the truth of your divinity. Do not let your thoughts dis-empower you Jesus stated confidently, "all power is given unto me" He said I am going away from you in humanity but you shall do greater works than what I do in my human experience on earth.

Don't be fearful to be who you are, this is not about Christianization or any other religion. Others around you may not accept you for who you are, but connected with your Source h/she will be well pleased. Never seek approval and validation from other, no one who go against God's love can win. Know that you know who you are as a divine being living in a human tent.

The eternal being you are is hidden in that temporary tent call human body. Shift your thoughts from condescension and raise it to divine inspiration. Walk in-spirit and demonstrate the energy of God in you and dispel the enemy of your true identity. Be true to your changing tent that goes through a life cycle but remember the spirit in you have one cycle eternal life. The soul is the observer of the tent you live in and energize you to walk in the spirit and not fulfill the fleshly prompting. The New Testament says "your body is the temple of the living God".

For changes to take place, in your life and the lives of others, it is a mental proposition and a mental reposition of your thoughts. It is an exercise of noble and active ideas of mind, heart and soul. Thinking is a divine perpetual brainstorming that enables you to be vigilant of the adversary of your divine soul. Thinking is the vehicle of constructive and credible change.

Changes gives birth to new actions, new thinking and new inspired inventions. Just one person thought to decide not be fenced in by rules, inject lasting changes to traditions and prejudice.

In 1831 in the time of slavery in the West Indies, Sam Sharpe set out to create a strike on the British plantations in western Jamaica. The slaves were instructed by this Baptist Deacon not to work until wages was instituted. This was revolutionary thinking out of the box of British dominance. Deacon Sam Sharpe refused to be fenced in by immoral rules and injustice. This action creates the emergence of the end of slavery in the British colonial system. Change the enslavement of the human dominance and reach in your inner and higher self. You will make an awakening difference that shift the human focus to divine inspiration.

The pages of history are "alive" with different individuals with a shift in thinking that burst new meaning to many lives. On November 8, 1946 in Nova Scotia Canada, Viola Desmond a black Halifax woman stopped by the Roseland Theatre to watch a movie. She was told that she could not sit downstairs because that space was reserve for whites only. She was not willing to be fenced in by immoral rules and human ego. Deep in her thoughts in a divine place she resolved, "not today! I am sitting right here". The Manger called the police to enforce the immoral rules plastered with open prejudice that states that black must sit in the balcony upstairs. That rule was crafted in the human ego called racism.

She refused to move from the seat. The heartless confrontation escalated. The police dragged her out of the movie theatre like a criminal and arrested her. Viola Desmond, from the inner recesses of her soul she was inspired to make that shift that transcend human rules. Ten years later segregation formally ended in Nova Scotia Canada. She starts and bring life to a discussion for equality.

Viola Desmond shift her thinking and was inspired by the God in her on that day in November 1946. She raised others to consciousness that isolating people because of the colour of their skin was immoral. In 2010 the Province of Nova Scotia apologized and pardon Viola Desmond. They were enforcing immoral prejudice unfair human ego rules. Shift the way you think and it can give birth to lasting change to you and your neighbors. It will spur that unconditional love of neighbors as yourself.

In the 1960s the rules in the United States of America was blatantly clear that blacks were to ride at the back of the bus. Rosa Parkes refuse to obey that unjust rule and sat at the front of the bus. Her transformational thinking to change this prejudice brought lasting changes to the rules. These kinds of inspirational stance will evoke changes that can only come about through divine commitment that is coming from your higher self. I am not here saying that they were member of some church or any other movement or religion. The frustration of injustice clearly was at work in the resolve of Rosa parks and the others mentioned above. Under these psychological sufferings the human reached it limit. When the human reached the divine in silence; the God who they are an extension of inspired them to act from their higher self.

Sam Sharpe, Viola Desmond and Rosa Parkes and may others because they act outside of their human boundary and was inspired by their divinity brought transformation and revolutionary changes to systems that was acting unjustly. Or at the least they start the journey towards equality and justice for all.

Change the way you think and it will bring irrevocable revolutionary changes in your life and that of your fellowman. The way to know love for yourself and not through any other is to be willing the listen to the silent presence in your inner being. From that inner discovery you will be inspired to give love for the benefit of your neighbors some who you have never met. Many of the freedom fighters did not live to experience the result of the sacrifice the made but they commence the journey. They leave the human tent before their transformational leadership to a change process that is still active today.

Martin Luther King Jr. as an African American Civil Rights icon is celebrated globally because of his inspired thinking strategies. That strategy of freedom and justice through peace, non-violence and meekness. Every lasting change in the history of the universe is brought to life from an inspired divine thinker. Divine thinking supersedes legislative power and penetrate legislators.

Theses resolves and thinking that enable you to love unconditionally because the natural man cannot love without conditions. These freedom fighters did not live long enough to reap the fruit of their resolve for changes but they did it at the risk of losing their own lives for others. However, their active engagement to bring about equality for all remains indelible in heart and lives globally.

The men and woman who blaze the trail for justice and equality, to stop slavery, prejudices and civil rights, does it with enthusiasm – the God in them was active. They shift their thinking to demolish the immoral and human egotistical rules. They set themselves in the political and social firing line to manifest fundamental changes. The system of the day can be challenge from a divine imperative because love is the ultimate way to real change. The bible said "one shall put a thousand to flight and two ten thousand". AS I have stated before in this book every problem needs divine solution.

George William Gordon, Deacon Paul Bogle and Reverend Martin Luther King Jr. were killed for their accomplishment. They loved their country and their people as a result of that inspiration they were willing even to die for that cause. God did the same through Jesus. These freedom fighters, men and women were not pressured to do what they did, they were inspired to action. Their indelible divine influence has imprinted the pages of history for freedom and equality. It was this intangible and weightless part of Marcus Mosiah Garvey that is called him to liberate the minds of people in addition their freedom from inequity and sufferings. He was inspired to fight with enthusiasm "the God In him" for a people who did not know adequately their history and culture. A people lost in an identity crisis if you are lost in an identity crisis, you can emancipate yourself through divine acknowledgement.

The shift in thinking of this black St. Ann born Jamaican, who travelled to England, United States and Canada to promote equality for all mankind was a soul movement. His divine shift in thinking, after great insight and observation connected to his source/God led him to start the UNIA - United Negro Improvement Association movement. This movement took on international fervor among blacks in the Americas and the Caribbean. He was committed to black movement to transform the economic and social possibilities for black people.

These outstanding life missionaries knew from their higher self that you were not born to suffer human abuse. You were Born as divine force to live your purpose for what God created you to be. The most amazing things happens when you trust that divine God who dwells in you. Allow this inner light in you to guide you to true inspiration.

Change the way you think and it will change you and change the world you live in. You are a divine being living in a human housing. Don't feel guilty to change those beliefs that enslaved you by a human external chain. You may acquire them from tradition, social connections, religion or political persuasion but if they don't serve your divine fullness. Those beliefs that do not bring you peace and love to and for your neighbor discard them.

Never let what happen in the past hold you hostage. These men and women had painful realities in the past. They reached into their higher self and saw potentialities and move with decisive actions to actualized their thoughts. Treasure your present, it is the only resource you have, it is call 'now'.

Don't live for human approval, you will become a slave to your humanity and not your true self. Review your inner divine rules before you make rules for others. Some rules are immoral filled with ego and energized by prejudice. Your circumstances of life are your teacher that will drive you to your divine source. There is no greater and more fulfilling experience in life than knowing you are connected to God in you. Define your own realities, they are building block to teach you something you did not know. The unconditionally loving silent divine intelligence abides within you. Everything that you believe you inherit from others can be discarded and evoke a deeper connection with your divinity. Know that divinity is everywhere and inside every human being.

Weigh your beliefs and traditional inheritance if they serve well. Know who you are in the divine plan of your source and meditate on His truth. Let knowing become a part of your determination and be ready to reengage the divine connection. Stand up for who you are and the purpose of your existence. Be open to give up human ego and be guided by your higher divine self. The damage in your life needs love to bring healing and transformation.

Be willing to love others without being judgmental. Pursue love in every listening exercise. Never let ego be a part of your listening skills. Know that love is non-threatening ingredient in listening to others regarding their situations. Allow your loved ones, family and friends to be who they are. Never try to make them to be who they are not. Never judge them if they disagree with you or your standard, values, religion or morality; Just love them unconditionally.

Your divine self is higher than your human self it will enable you to accomplish the unpredictable. Release every anger or hate from your inner being. Throw out any resentment in you it does not matter how it gets there. Resentment only hurt the carrier it will not bring value to your life. See the divine intelligence in the reasons to have the resentment and love the person or persons who create the reasons for any resentment. Make love the theme and philosophy of your existence, it will enlighten and elevate you above any existing condition.

There is a divine energy working inside you. Try create a realm of possibility in you through divine consciousness. Declare from your innermost being that you will have resentment for no one. Cultivate a spirit of meekness in your inner being. Live life in its fullness of your divinity and you will no longer live in the survival realm. This is the thinking and action energy that will enable you to make meaningful changes to your circumstances. In other words, you are making a covenant with yourself that will sustain you for life in this human body.

We can always identify with some kind of predicament. Every predicament needs more than human energy to advance from it. Predicament means there is no human solution; no human way out. It could be an addiction or anything that is humanly impossible. Reconstructing of your thinking is like becoming like a little child that see only possibilities manifesting through their parents, teachers and guardians. This childlike thinking revokes the restrictions and allow you to reinvent your future through transformational divine energy. If you find yourself with an intensified desire that you just cannot control, just turn that light to your inner-self. The use of love which is love for self and others is an invisible force for good. It is the energy of resolution of the deepest emotional, social, physical and psychological scars.

Search your inner self for the greatest divine energy that mystical and profound God knowledge. That exist before you were formed in your mother's womb. Be cognizant that your source is that present inner divine energy that is your help in times of trouble. It is an inspirational energy that brings the best out of who you are to face your moment of challenge.

This spiritual silence of reinventing yourself with transformational insight is the vehicle that transport you to see the perfection in the imperfection. There might be some deep hurt in you that cause immense emotional pains and anguish. It will seem justified to be angry with the person or persons that inflict that hurt. They may even be unsympathetic and will not acknowledge that they have done you wrong. May be in the name of religion, politics or any other self-promoting reasons they are satisfied with their actions.

Free yourself from the human ego and stand in the peace and freedom of your divine soul. Put your divine thought in motion and declare possibilities because with God all things are possible.

Let me tell you! there is an inner divine energy that can completely deal with your hurts comprehensively. In order to make this divine paradigm shift this feeling of being let down and being a victim must be discarded. Be still and look deeply within and embrace your divinity. Remove from believing about the divine presence of God to knowing that God is presence in you. It requires a shift of thinking from believing to knowing. Knowing is more than a mere belief that is handed down to you. This is now in the realm of experiencing and encountering invisible divine spirit. That loving gentle energy is on the inside of the universal human being guiding you always. Enter into a place within yourself and find that active soul energy that brings transformation.

You have absolutely no benefit to have resentment or to pursue revenge. Ego will tell you that resentment and revenge is your only tool to exonerate you from your hurt. Ego robs you of who you are and put humanity above divinity. Find the secret of soul empowerment that can be found when you are willing to look deep within. As you were born into the world in your human heritage, you have divine heritage to develop this winning strategy to act outside of your ego.

MEEKNESS AND KINDNESS

Meekness and kindness are scoffed at in many cases as weakness. Jesus said the "meek will inherit the earth". You will find freedom and peace when you let go of ego and aspire to be driven by divine energy. Your spiritual accomplishment and winning strategies are not attained through ego. Through compassionate calmness and gentleness, you will reach the deepest sense of completion and wholeness. The multiplicity of hurts and challenges in relationships or any other situations in your life must come into a heart of deep love. Meekness and love will magnetize your painful situations that exceeds your human control to that gentle inner you.

Paul said in the New Testament "Be kind one to another, loving one another, tender hearted as God in Christ forgave you" Ephesians 4:32. Ego is a demonstration of self-seeking goals, while love accentuates who we truly are as divine being living in an earthly temporary tabernacle call body. Take a breath and pay some attention to the knocking for entry to go inside. The inner higher divine self is the most ignored. We are so busy seeking outer ego solutions we ignore the beckoning of the heart for loving healing solutions.

Make every effort to throw your hand in the air and surrender your ego. There is a higher place to operate from than through ego. Ego is the wounded part of you that collects all the debris negative experiences where we felt disrespected and let down. It contains and retains all these dark moments where we were un recognized pushed aside. Ego tends to tell you that you are damaged and rejected so you must fight for you right and show you authority. It rules out the reality that your experiences and encounters was lessons for your greater inner good.

Reach into your innermost being and open that door on the inside of you to replace ego with divine compassion. The overwhelming force that will always move from victory to victory over ego is love. God is love, you are love and you are His beloved.

Fulfill who you are in the battleground where evil and hate seems to be taking preeminence. There is a higher and greater clarity to life if you let your soul take the place of your ego. Ego will steal away the truth of your divine self. Ego has a false set of guidelines of securing recognition and respect. Your soul allows you to live with unconditional love. On the other hand, your ego promote self to gain recognition and respect. We are not better than anyone else or is other's better than you we are all equal by God's standard. The first order of recognition and respect involve everyone doing to others as to yourself. We all should show regards and respect to each other, parent to children, employer to employee, friends to friends etc.

The other person opinion should be respected. You may not agree with it you should try not to take it personal. We all can see and interpret things differently. Living in a world where being different is scoffed at criticized you should endeavor to embrace diversity. Differences allows for creativity and diverse ideas, not imposing on others to meek your expectations.

To exist in an abstract a universe with the same theory about reality would be stagnant and uninteresting. If people share a different belief system whether religion or politics you should be open to listen to them without being judgmental. There is this overreaching way of thinking that penetrates our world; where if others don't wear the same labels as yours or see their spirituality as you do, there is the tendency to judge them based on your conviction. In the bible it clearly states that you should not judge others in respect meat and drink and with regards to holy days nor the sabbath day.

The food you eat, what you wear and how you worship and carry out certain religious rituals is not the prescription for living. The Spirit is the source of divine motivation and the enabler of fulfilling God's purpose.

When Rosa Parks, the black American woman who I mentioned before refuse to give up her seat in the bus. She knew the rules were immoral. She did not consult with any one on the bus to get their opinion. There were people on the bus who did not share her opinion and was not in agreement with her. However, she made it known based on her individual conviction and became the catalysis of civil rights in America. Her story has made world history and become many people's story. She was executing her divine action to impacted the life of generations to come. We all has a role to play in our unique way.

Your inspiration cannot be developed by human innovation and evocation. Your human body is just the vehicle to transport that divine energy. The world was created out of nothing we are co-workers with God. It is the spirit that gives life. In order for you to create anything you must start from a place of thinking. Your thoughts is the place of nothing to take action it is a powerful silence within. St. Paul said in the New Testament "that which is seen hath not come from that which doth appear". The existence of everything in the world has it origin in the spirit realm inside of humanity. It is from the invisible source which has no limitations all things come into existence.

Living in the world of your divinity is the world of spirit. You are endowed with inspiration; which means, "in spirit". There is spiritual myopia in our world. We are set to believe in this age that everything must be scientifically balance. There are inspirational and transformational actions that the human will not be able de-mystify. There is the need sometimes to shift the emphasis from science and logics to being inspired and operate in-spirit. I am not making an opposition to science because is real.

The source of everything is from God and you are God's work-man-ship. You are living from a divine conviction where you transcend the limitations. Extraordinary thoughts will develop and divine direction will saturate your being and ideas becomes actions. Talents will not be buried and faith will become active as you evoke your higher self. You will get a profound insight and understanding that the universe was formed by God's command.

What is seen was not made out of what was visible its divine action. That dormant force that is restrained by your human being will come alive in you. It is deep in your soul with full unhindered access to God's unlimited resources to create active changes. To manifest this reality, you need to migrate to the world of spirit and don't see money, ego or any other thing be obstacles.

Hebrew 11:3 states "By faith we understand that the universe was formed at God's command, so that what is seen was not made out of what was visible".

You must strive to change the inner conversation from abstract to transformational driving energy. You can broadcast from a more prolific frequency that is limitless. You have access to divine resources. In this human oriented life, the whole human race is competing with the same idea. That idea of human limitations, you are divine, infinite, eternal and limitless. You need to leave ego village with the same people with the same message and mentality. Advance to the freeway of divine intelligence and conscious, to stop competing with each other in the border of their humanity. You must enter into a place of inspiration that allow you to complement each other rather than competing. This is called transformation, that is to operate outside of your humanity.

When you transform the way you think, all things are possible with the source. The source of the spring water is the spring. It doesn't matter how far the water flows. If you bottle the water and ship it across the globe, the source of the water is still that particular spring.

It does not matter where we go, what we do, God still remains our divine source connected by our soul. Jesus used an allegory or parable to convey this profound truth 'I am the true vine, ye are the branches. The branches cannot be different from the vine. The vine is the source from which the branches gets its energy and possibilities to bear fruit. Therefore, you are divine being, that's the connection to God! but living in a human tent.

You are one with the father, the source even as Jesus said He and His father is one. You cannot be different; God sees perfection in all of us because he breathes in us and sees Himself in us.

According to the gospel, when Jesus came to John to be baptized, John complained "I need to be baptized by you. Jesus said, John let it be so now, it is the right thing to do to fulfill all righteousness". After the baptism

God said "I am well pleased". God sees Jesus in his divine perfection although He was clothed in a human body. God looks at your divinity and see perfection in you although your human body is changing and deteriorating and will die.

God saw the long human road that Jesus will go through. He saw his Gethsemane experience; his arrest; and trial before the authorities. Peter dis-own him, soldiers mocked him; they crucified him. God sees victory through all these ordeals. He saw his divine perfection and said "I am well pleased".

God is saying, 'I see ahead and know all your encounters, but I see your divine soul that will never change and is invisible in contrast to your human tent that will decay. If you go to your source and say 'I am limited, I don't have, He will be baffled because He said "I provided all things for you that pertain to life and Godliness". God is saying to you, you are divine; you are a part of me; I will supply all you need; and my grace is adequate.

Let us be what our divine source is. How to fulfill that role? Love him with all your heart, mind, soul and strength and your neighbor as yourself. You cannot be different from your source you are divine. Send love in the universe. Love know no border. Love build no walls.

Think like your source/God, He sees you in divine perfection. God is love; love is God; you are a part of God. You are not your own, you are bought with a price and you are interdependent. God sends love where hate exist in huge volume. God so love, he came to us through humanity by Jesus the Messiah. God send His son so that through love the whole universe can be rescued from hate. Love is the one and only energy that can bring true change to all people.

Life possibilities move to action when you engage in active love of God with who you are and love your neighbor as yourself. Love evoke and cultivate divine conversation which becomes a divine way of life.

Love cannot be acted it is manifested to actions. When love is absent from our human relationships, it is just an academic exercise. Praying can only be generated from a divine soul because prayer is a divine conversation. Prayer is a divine dialogue that transcend the human confinement and limitations. Divine love makes you ready to take on the impossible.

Divine love prepares you to produce results outside your reality, like loving your enemies. When divine love become your theme and motivation the opening that inner and higher self becomes a successful reality of life.

Success if not measured by your temporal achievements. Success is that inner feedback you are getting from that divine conversation you are having with your source/God.

Love must be your compelling motive to serve rather than to be served. Carefully reflect on why you are here. This kind of love cannot be accomplished with your human power. Transformation that comes from the inner you are the means to accomplish true love. Break free from your human limitations. You are more spirit than flesh and more divine than human. You are made in the image of God your source. He knew you before you were formed in your mother's womb,

Do not focus on your limitations. You can love like God love. He said the love commandment is the premium because on it hangs all the other commandments. Dispel guilt from your being, it will immobilize you. Your debts are fully paid up by love, therefore love is now free to give away.

Treasure your present and continuous freedom through divine love. Remember you cannot change what happen in the past. You cannot fix what happen in the past. Live in the love of the now and stop getting pre-occupied with your past. People will label you base on what they know about your past. Never accept any imposed labels only know yourself through divine love.

Jesus lived His life through loving service. He was gentle, he was kind, he was meek and selfless. He was human being, living out his divinity. We must enter into our inner-self and strive to be of service to others. Be gentle, kind, meek and selfless. We too can live in our divinity though we are clothed in humanity. If your life is a positive reference and a positive influence you are living your divinity.

Our existence is to offer divine unconditional love to all. To grasped the secret of satisfaction and prosperity you must be inspired and find it in your divine self. Having a lot of human gains will not offer you true satisfaction. The things that happen outside of your true identity does not determine who you are. You are a divine creation of your God.

The wholesomeness of who you are is inside of your human tent dwelling in silence. To bring out the real you are through inspiration (in-spirit). Every invention give birth through inspiration. Whether you agree or disagree with the contents of this book, it was birthed through inspiration.

Empowerment is to know that external forces are not the determinant factor that make you who you are. You are a divine being made into the image of God. The entire universe without boundaries is a vehicle for your good and well-being. God give all things to us for life and godliness. In the peaceful quietness of our souls we discover constantly God in his/her divine presence.

The electricity that flows through our dwelling; is like that spiritual current that flows through our body. It is unseen, intangible but it illuminates and energized us for good. We have that priceless flow of divine energy flowing through our innermost being. This divine energy illuminates our surroundings. Jesus said "you are the light of the world".

Negativity and judgement of others because they are different, behave different, worship different will darken our soul from being the light. We must shift from form to spirit to fulfill who we are as life giving divine creature. Surrendering to our divine self is an act of your will - your inner and higher self. Let go of your human limitation and be free in your divine self. Jesus said through his human grief and agonizing experience; "If it is possible, let this cup/agony past from me, but nevertheless, not my human will be done but your divine will be done".

"My soul is exceedingly sorrowful even unto death" said Jesus. Your soul, that divine place in your being is the entry door to your miracle. Forgiveness is the ability to give love even in agonizing circumstances. Love is this unconditional divine energy that ignites the universe. Love is giving and it has nothing to do with what you receive in return. Unconditional love when you live it and give it all things are possible. It is a constant and continuous thought process matter of the heart. We have that divine inspiration flowing through us that makes love possible.

The ultimate essence and purpose of life is to love. The energy of love to love yourself and love others will result in overwhelming peace and profound joy. Any other motivation will soon bring turmoil that is set to destroy and destabilize relationships.

Transcend rituals and tradition and take a close divine look at the flood of religious labels and dogmas. These labels and dogmas are motivated by human ego. Be part of the divine organism that promote the God in you who is love. This divine organism should be a movement that manifest the invisible intangible weightless soul.

The motivation is to let your life be a benediction of love. It must bear a transforming energy that have life giving enrichment. The operations must evoke a divine frequency with a purpose much bigger than you. These labels, beliefs and tradition to a large extent can be distractions. Your life must be bursting with inspiration of love that' the highest and ultimate goal in life. That is attainable through surrendering the human ego and complete and yielding to your divinity. God gave us direct connection to his divine character as an extension of his divine love. Just allow your connection to be there, not through religion and religiosity but through divine Emanuel consciousness.

Jesus in his humanity speaking from his divinity states, the following in the New Testament; "You study the scriptures diligently because you think that in them you have eternal life. These are the very scriptures that testify of me yet you refuse to come to me to have life…John 5:39-40. I receive no praise honor from man. I am divine, I can only receive honor through divinity".

Your humanity is only a temporary housing called body. This human encasement deteriorates and subject to decay. Honor me through your divine self, I am in you. You must let go the ego that generate thy hyper religious competitiveness. You must open the door on your inside and reach to your higher self and be the God in you. The divine self will bring transformation to all through deep and intimate connection.

Jesus said "I do not receive honor from men" that is from the human self. I only come to identify with you in humanity for you to identify with me in divinity. The knowing of connection to God is what bring about the joy of worry-free living. That knowledge engages the silent divine presence that effortlessly flow from your innermost being. From this divine higher self, you unfold the Source of love which is who you are as an extension of God.

Your mandate is to love God with all your heart, mind, strength and soul and your neighbor as yourself. I came in the name of the father, we are on. That is the divine position I represent. Jesus came in humanity to identify with your limitations and direct you to your divine self. It is immensely possible to give prominence to your divinity. Jesus said in John 5:43 "I come in my father's name; and you do not accept me; but if someone else come in his name you will…

You must love God with all your heart, all your strength, all you might, all your soul and love your fellowmen as yourself. The love formula dwells in your soul. If you look to your humanity for that burst of love, you are looking in the wrong direction. Start an exploration of your inner self to find peace and joy in silence. Healing and solutions to life's distractions/problems in your life is inside of you.

Think divine, live divine; let the unconditional love flame burn inside of you. The human will try to penetrate your thoughts with, you can't; You are weak; 'You are not worthy'; 'You was born like this and it runs into your family'. Paul in the New Testament said - I can do all things through the divine source who enabled me. We have to be transformed by renewed thinking. Think possibilities; think love; think victory over defeat. What you think is what you become, " as you think in your heart, so are you".

Never tell yourself that you have a right to live angry, anxious and antagonistic. It doesn't matter the circumstances you can rise above it and live in your higher self. If you fill yourself with these things those things will come out in your life. What you put in you will automatically come out especially when you are confronted with challenges.

GOD WITH US

The term "God with us" is God present in human body. God came to us, clothed in humanity but He is always present with us in His divinity. Meaning he was present in us before He came in human form, born through a woman as all of us came to earth. Before we were formed in our mother's womb, He knew us. God with us is personal and divine and He promised never to leave us nor forsake us. Never means- "at no time in the past or future, or on no occasion, not ever".

Micah 5:2 states "You Bethlehem Ephrathah; though you are small among the clan of Judah; out of you will come for me one who will be ruler over Israel; whose origin are from old, from ancient of time' – before you were formed in your mother's womb, I knew you. We all are from ancient time; our origin is from old without beginning and without end. We are divine weightless, invisible eternal being as well as human being with physical body.

You might be an obscurity like a dead stump and passed over and passed over because of your color or status; by human but I am with you and I have plans for you. You are chosen of me; 'you are royal priesthood; you are a divine and a holy clan; you are the apple of my eye; you are the head and not the tail. The dryness, the aridity of the stump seems hopeless and useless but the shoot will spring up when you yield to your divine origin.

Many todays believe it is impossible for God to become man... Exodus 20:4 said, "don't make for yourself any idols....". My words to you now is not to create any graven image because God dwells in you in that human housing; God with us – within. In many pages of scripture God communicates with his people in human form through their divinity. Think of Abraham who welcomed three strangers in his tent at Mamre. The bible said the Lord appeared to Abraham (Genesis 13:18). Consider Jacob who wrestle all night with God and called the place "Peniel" – meaning " I have seen God face to face". Remember Moses who He communicate with through the burning bush. God is always in us; those were his visible appearances in different forms.

When tribes of Israel decided to be ruled by kings like other nations, God explained to the Prophet Samuel that this is a choice of human lordship over divine leadership. (1 Samuel 8:7). What is your choice today, will determine your outcome; - Humanity or Divinity? After Saul's disastrous rule, David received a promised from Nathan that David's throne and lineage will be established forever – 'God with us. The promised explained in Isaiah 9:6-7 although was a stump with massive unattractive root system it was inevitable that it must be established upon the earth and in heaven. Even if you feel unrecognized, unattractive or even don't believe it, you are still an extension of God. In that exist the secret of humanity to manifest divinity. "You are a promise; You are a tremendous possibility" when you live to you higher self. It is not the form that you must aspire to emulate to be or to be like everybody else. You should align yourself to the formidable source that you are inevitably a part of. He is able to keep you from falling, to present faultless with exceeding joy in His presence. You may be different from the religious prescription from what you are told or come to believe; you unavoidably have God; living in you. Only Him know you secrets and all your, life's politics, purposes and problems.

There is no political solution to any problem in this vast and wonderful universe that was created by God in perfection. Political fix was the hope of Israel when they demanded a human king over God's divine order, clearly it did not work. It increases the demand and burden on the people. If you try to use human strategies and human leadership to bring solutions to our world, it will result in chaos and confusion. In Isaiah 9:6 it states; "For unto us a child is born, a son is given and the government will be on his shoulder". We are not hopeless when we make God active in us. The plumb line of reasoning cannot comprehend it. Hermeneutics cannot explain it. The learned scholars cannot de-mystify it, God is in us!

Show love to a thousand generation. Listen to everyone without judgement and prejudice then you will not mis-use the name of God/ Love. Deuteronomy 16:5 "Love the Lord your God with all your heart, and with all your soul and with all your strength'. He added, let it be upon your heart …. Impress them on your children". Talk about love when you sit at home; talk about love when you walk along the road; talk about love when you lie down and when you get up. Matthew 22:35 Jesus aid "love the Lord your God with all your heart and with all your soul and with all your mind'. This is the first and greatest commandment and the second is like it; Love your neighbor as yourself". With everything else written and spoken hold on these two, actions. Practice them with and in all your life.

Look nowhere else for who you really are but inside of you. Jesus said 'I am the door' – just open the door on your inside. It is that divine self that is called a living soul connected to source. Do not live as a mere human being it is an illusion to live as just flesh. There is a light within you, it is call divine intelligence it can show you your true image and essence.

Jesus said "we are the light of the world", just like he was in his human stay on earth, He illuminate the world. You are the shining light of the world living in a human being. Our divinity enables us to confront any darkness and conquer any vicissitudes. This is what you want in your divine self – to fulfill your divine assignment and divine purpose.

A limitless and fearless soul is that divine inner you that do not focus on what you have. God asked Moses 'what is that you have in your hand?' Moses had a mere rod but God said 'Use it!' That fearless divine soul in you is saying "Use what you have". There is an indefinable you. This indefinable you are infinite and changeless. Place your thoughts in harmony with your source/God.

You have a key to who you are, that key can open only one door and that door is installed in your inner-self. Opening this door on your inside will expose you through divine transformation to make a positive impact in this universe. Opening this door of your supreme self will give you a leap over your limitation. This opening will show you how to love unconditionally, to love the loveless, to love the haters.

Now you are operating outside of your human being and walking in the spirit. You are now placed in the presence of your source. Think divine thoughts and get divine results. This opening of your inner door to your soul will awaken your divine thinking. Your supernatural surrender enlightens you to love your enemies. You will transcend human limitations and evoke a vibration of freedom and peace without fear that will dramatically change your composure to life in its fullness. Life can be a joyful encounter cemented with divine empowerment even in the prison of circumstances.

In the book of Philippians in the New Testament, Paul was in detention and he wrote to some saints in Philippi he gave an account of who the saints were. He told them that he was grateful for the gifts and help they offered him while he was in detention. He told them to be joyful in all circumstances. Make joy your disposition. He was telling the people in the congregation at Philippi to literally imitate the Christ humility as Christ manifest his divinity while living as a human. He highlighted the fact that you should be encouraged that you and Christ share unity of identity.

Paul said be comforted by this truth that operates from His love and divine fellowship with the spirit. Paul stated that your like mindedness with Christ make your joy complete. Christ thought it not robbery to be equal with God. To say you have the same mind is not blasphemy – it is your true soul identity. He said you must have the same love as Christ demonstrated in his human experience, placing his divinity in prominence.

The apostle wrote "do nothing out of selfish ambition or vain glory but of humility and esteem others". Do not look to your own interest but to others interest. Your attitude should be the same as that of Christ who being in nature of God did not consider equality with God something to be grasped. Jesus was fully God in human housing temporarily. He took on humanity with all the appearance of a man. He humbles himself and became obedient, even to death on a cross.

Although you may not be able to explain your divinity rationally, your spiritual intuitions are created by divine spirit. Have confidence and affirm your divine self without doubt. It is not to boast and become pretentious but to declare who you really are in this world. With these truths of who you are as a divine being, works instinctively in you. You will manifest divine qualities and view the worlds through a divine lens. This will allow you to have profound insight, biblical language like " All things works together for good" give you divine perspective of the world with less complexity. For it is God who works in you to will and act according to his good pleasure.

Solomon in the Old Testament after exploring a wide variety of life's experiences. He came to one conclusion that the whole duty of man is to serve God and keep His commandments. The first and greatest commandments as I stated before; is to "Love God with all you heart, all your strength, all your mind and your neighbor as yourself." God want us to love and serve others. Human beings tend to seek approval of men or validation from others. You must be your validator you must know who you are than others. You can make yourself known as a divine resource for consultation.

They also tell us that we are what we achieved in life. God say we are to be who he called us to be and that is love. Conscious contact with God is divine and indivisible. Replace all your labels with your limitless reality that you are a divine being. You can change the way you think of yourself. The greatest validator is your divine wisdom, that will be the pre-requisite before your actions. Reinforce your knowledge that you are more a diving being than a human being. Your soul and divinity are internal and invisible. Let this mind be in you that was also in Christ Jesus who thought it not robbery to be equal with God.

God is everywhere, therefore there is no place where he is not present. God is your source and your body is the temple of God. Place ego on the outer court of who you are and enter into the inner court of who you are created in the image of God to be. You are a soul that is invisible, eternal weightless and limitless.

Take responsibility for who you are, and don't wait on men's approval. You already have God's approval, of you as a divine being living in a human tent. Try not to see your co-workers; your community; your kinsmen as acting against you. See God in all things and in all human beings. Know that no one came into this world by accident. They are all a part of God's divine plan from before they were conceived in their mother's womb.

Being divine doesn't means you are above or better than anyone. we are all divine, created in the image of God. If you go around lesser than who you are, you will accept people opinion of who you are. Trust your divine insights and use them to serve others, not to manipulate or exploit others. Don't go around being angry because of other people's opinion of you. Then you are not living up to your true self. Thoughts of anger and hate dis-empower you. Thoughts of self-confidence, love, joy and peace empower you.

Jesus said in the gospel 'even the least amount you can do all I have done and even greater things. Stop living in denial of who you are. You are not a mere human being. God is a spirit and we must worship in him by spirit and in spirit. God is love and He gave away what he is. If you have love inside of you, naturally you will give it away. God so love that he gave himself to the world. If we so love, it will be natural for us to give it to the world. On the other side, if we practice hate, anger and unforgiveness that is what we will give away. Love is in abundance in our soul. We can give it away effortlessly because we are fill with it. Help others to understand that your divine thinking is to build and not to tear down. Let your divine thinking strategies be to consider others while living out your divinity above your humanity.

"AS A MAN THINKETH IN HIS HEART SO IS HE"-PROVERB 23:7

-The End-

www.ingramcontent.com/pod-product-compliance
Lightning Source LLC
Chambersburg PA
CBHW021631120626
46545CB00002B/487